Inside Abu Ghraib

Inside Abu Ghraib

*Memoirs of Two U.S. Military
Intelligence Officers*

WILLIAM EDWARDS,
ROBERT P. WALTERS, JR.,
and PAUL ZANON

McFarland & Company, Inc., Publishers
Jefferson, North Carolina

Library of Congress Cataloguing-in-Publication Data

Names: Edwards, William, 1967– author. | Walters, Robert P., 1961– author. | Zanon, Paul, author.
Title: Inside Abu Ghraib : memoirs of two U.S. military intelligence officers / William Edwards, Robert P. Walters, Jr. and Paul Zanon.
Description: Jefferson, North Carolina : McFarland & Company, Inc., Publishers, 2021 | Includes index.
Identifiers: LCCN 2021047581 | ISBN 9781476686738 (paperback : acid free paper) ∞
ISBN 9781476644554 (ebook)
Subjects: LCSH: Abu Ghraib Prison. | Iraq War, 2003–2011—Prisoners and prisons, American. | Walters, Robert P., 1961– | Edwards, William, 1967– | United States. Army. Military Intelligence Battalion, 165th—Biography. | United States. Army—Officers—Biography. | United States. Army.—Military life. | Prisons—Iraq—Social conditions. | Iraq War, 2003–2011—Personal narratives, American. | BISAC: HISTORY / Military / Iraq War (2003–2011)
Classification: LCC DS79.76 .E26 2021 | DDC 956.7044/30922 [B]—dc23
LC record available at https://lccn.loc.gov/2021047581

British Library cataloguing data are available

ISBN (print) 978-1-4766-8673-8
ISBN (ebook) 978-1-4766-4455-4

Front cover images: Makeshift security tower overlooking detainees aimlessly walking around the compound (William Edwards collection); LTC Walters briefing the troops—No change to mission (William Edwards collection); Major Edwards observing the cells which had been used for detainees on death row in Abu Ghraib (Mike Flentie collection)

Printed in the United States of America

McFarland & Company, Inc., Publishers
  Box 611, Jefferson, North Carolina 28640
    www.mcfarlandpub.com

To the many family members who
selflessly sacrifice and steadfastly
support their soldier.

Acknowledgments

A big thanks goes to Romeo Qureishi, Mickie Willams, Mike Flentie for taking the time to add some anecdotal color to this book, and to John Moore for facilitating the introduction between Colonel William Edwards, Major General Robert P. Walters , Jr., and Paul Zanon.

Special thanks to Nancy Walters, Daytona Erkan and Martina Malek (wife and daughters of General Walters) and Dana Edwards, Madeline Edwards and Elise Edwards (wife and children of Colonel Edwards).

Last but not least, a special mention goes to Colonel Edwards and General Walters from Paul Zanon for taking numerous months to recall one of the most poignant episodes of their lives so candidly.

Table of Contents

Acknowledgments   vi

A Note from the Department of Defense   ix

Preface   1

The Protagonists: Boys to Men   3

Introduction: A Bad Vibe   9

Prologue: Ambushed   12

  1. The Day That Changed the World   19

  2. The Other Theater   22

  3. When Bill Met Bob   28

  4. Who Let the Dogs Out?   35

  5. Summer of 2003   39

  6. Call to Action   43

  7. Embrace the Suck   48

  8. Reconnaissance   59

  9. Groundwork   68

10. Beyond the Pale   81

11. Resident Nightingale   90

12. Managing Death   94

13. Locally Sourced   102

14. Beef Jerky   111

15. Feeding Time at Abu Ghraib   117

16. Christmas Day   124

Table of Contents

17. It's Good to Talk   134

18. Under Fire   142

19. So Long Abu Ghraib   156

20. "That" Disk   167

21. Home Time   175

22. Child's Perspective   179

23. Adjustment   188

24. Clocking Out   195

Index   213

A Note from the Department of Defense

The views expressed in this publication are those of the author and do not necessarily reflect the official policy or position of the Department of Defense or the U.S. government.

The public release clearance of this publication by the Department of Defense does not imply Department of Defense endorsement or factual accuracy of the material.

The soldier above all prays for peace, for it is the soldier who must suffer and bear the deepest wounds and scars of war. —Douglas MacArthur

Preface

A good friend of mine approached me and said, "Paul, I have a friend of mine who is a former high ranking U.S. Army officer called Bill and he has a friend called Bob, who is also a high ranking officer. They have served in Iraq and might wish to use their stories to form the basis of a book. I have no further information as I did not wish to pry." I thanked my friend and contacted Bill.

Writing a book is similar to a marriage inasmuch as you will be spending several months with the clients and it's essential that you all get along and have a warm platform of communication. Before committing to any book, I always request to have an in-depth conversation with the client, just to gauge whether I feel I can work with them long term. In less than five minutes, Bill gave me the whistle stop tour of his decorated military career, pinpointing some of the hair-raising moments from Abu Ghraib, and I instantly felt the sincerity and humility from the man. He then recommended a Zoom call with Bob.

On a parallel to Bill, Bob radiated with that similar warmth and honesty, again, sharing a few moments about Abu Ghraib, which confirmed the solid foundation for this book.

Putting aside the integrity of Bill and Bob, unique selling points are an essential factor of any manuscript. After shining a torch in a few corners and detailing a number of anecdotes which had previously not been publicized, Bob added one more gem: "Paul—There's a number of sources out there which always talk about the soldiers downrange; however, a unique aspect that needs highlighting is the role of the wives back at base and the effects on the families." Bob was right. I conducted extensive research and this kind of information mainly came in the form of formal papers, presenting qualitative and quantitative data. In essence, with very little direct dialogue from the spouses and children. After those initial two conversations with Bill and Bob, I knew we had a lot of fresh material to bring to the reader's table.

Working with military personnel has been a fantastic experience as they would always assist in any questions I had and any necessary bridges to facilitate peripheral interviews for research. It was essential to speak with certain key members of the 165th Military Intelligence Battalion and more poignantly, Bill and Bob's families. Within hours of requesting a detailed conversation with any of them, either Bill or Bob had set up the line of communication. That primary research is essential in bringing unique content to the table, but also adding color to existing anecdotes.

The writing process took around eight months from blank page to draft manuscript. I hope you enjoy walking in the shoes of Colonel William Edwards and Major General Robert P. Walters, Jr., as much as I did.

—Paul Zanon

◈◈◈

This book is a collection of personal memoirs from Major General Robert P. Walters, Jr., and Colonel William Edwards, presented with author Paul Zanon.

Speaking in the first person in a candid and often raw form, Lieutenant Colonel (LTC) Walters and Major Edwards (their ranks at the time of serving in Abu Ghraib) give their recollections of one of the most abhorrent prisons in history. Their narrative pulls no punches as it outlines their respective journeys to Iraq and their eventual deployment to Abu Ghraib in November 2003 under the banner of the 165th Military Intelligence Battalion.

Assigned the nearly impossible task of improving the security posture in unfathomable conditions, LTC Walters and Major Edwards shine a torch in a number of previously untouched corners, sharing firsthand anecdotes of death, destruction, but on occasions rib-tickling laughter. With extensive input from their wives and daughters and a healthy involvement from a small selection of officers who served alongside them, their story will evoke emotions on several levels.

The Protagonists

Boys to Men

"Try not to become a man of success, but rather to become a man of value."—Albert Einstein

Every soldier's route into the military is different. Many reach a crossroads in their life, some are inspired by their forefathers, others are a product of circumstance and some just think, "Let's give this a go. What's the worst that could happen?"

Major Edwards embarked on a highly decorated military career after playing a few years of college football: "That was my passion before I joined the Army. I was a pretty good wide receiver in a Southern California high school and then went on to play for California Lutheran University, the school I was eventually recruited by. California Lutheran was not a Division 1 school, which was the level of league play that one would need to be considered for play beyond the collegiate level.

"I realized real quick that I wasn't going to be a professional football player when I got there. I reported into the rookie camp, where they brought in all the freshmen, before they brought in all the sophomores, juniors and seniors on the team. They brought us in a week early and we had to go through a medical screening and all that type of stuff. I was about 5 ft 10 and weighed around 165 lbs at the time. I went to the physical test and I was waiting in the lobby and the doctor called me in and said, 'Are you the new kicker?' I said, 'What do you mean? I'm a receiver.' He replied, 'You're too small. You're going to get killed here. I need to speak to the weight coach, because we probably need to put about 25 lbs on you so that you can survive.'

"I played that year, left that school, transferred back to another school in Southern California, which was a junior college, and did quite well earning recognition in the league. I was then recruited by another University at the Division 1 level to be a possession receiver but I turned it down for my future career.

"I transferred to San Diego State University, which had about forty thousand students. I was walking past these white trailers on campus and there was a sign which said, 'Army Reserve Officers' Training Corps.' I thought, 'Hmmm. I'm going to walk in here and see what this is all about.' There was this guy named Captain Pete Ash, who is a good friend of mine to this very day. I walked in with shorts, t-shirt, flip-flops and a backpack and I said, 'What's the deal with this Army stuff?' Captain Pete Ash said, 'Take this ranger handbook and read it. If you like what's in it, come and see me.' I went home and saw it talked about rope bridges, jumping out of airplanes and I thought, 'This is really cool.' The next day I went back to Pete, and he put me in class. The rest is history. I never looked over my shoulder since. I joined the reserve officers' training corps in 1987 at the age of twenty and then I signed my enlistment contract in 1988."

Major Edwards as a high school football player (courtesy Chuck Bennett).

Despite a rather laid-back initial approach to joining the military, with Edwards' lineage, it seemed destiny was calling: "My dad is retired Navy. He was enlisted for twenty years and finished out his career at Naval Air station, Miramar, just outside of San Diego and was teaching the F14 Tomcat pilots, the ground simulators. My cousin was a marine in Saigon, Vietnam, my mom's brother, my uncle, was in Korea in the Army in the 1950's and I had another uncle who was a WWII veteran in the Pacific. Also, my great grandfather was a veteran in the Spanish-American war in 1898. So yeah. Maybe that walk past the reserve officers' training corps wasn't a complete accident."

It's a well-worn cliché, but behind every successful man is a strong woman. Edwards and his wife, Dana, first crossed paths in Berlin in 1990: "I was studying at the time and he had just moved into the apartment building I was staying at," she recalled, "but we never crossed paths or spoke. I remember my friend saying, 'I think he's American and he's some Army guy.'"

Edwards added: "When I arrived in Berlin the Army was in 'stoploss,' which meant no soldiers were allowed to move because of Desert Storm at the time. The unit was impacted because new people were arriving, but no one was rotating out, so housing was at a premium. The Army was renting apartments all over the city to put us in a place to live and I ended up sharing an apartment with a lab tech from our hospital out on the Wannsee lake. It just so happened Dana was living in the same building.

"The first time I saw Dana, she was walking past the American compound at Turner Barracks, and I said to a friend of mine, 'That's the girl I'm going to marry.' However, the first time I met her was at the German American Tennis Club where she worked."

Dana continued: "I was attending the Berlin Frei University as a student and at the time I had a student job working for a German firm, which did security for the Olympic stadium. However, the Berlin Wall had come down the year before which sent unemployment through the roof, so when I went to renew my working permit, they refused. I didn't know what to do, so I went to the U.S. consulate, and they said, 'Why don't you go to the civilian personnel office for the Army and see if they have a job?' They gave me the address and I ended up getting a job at the German American Tennis Club, checking people in, that sort of thing.

"Bill played tennis and he came in and started practicing with the tennis ball machine, trying to improve his strokes. He was regularly asking me out on a date, go to dinner, do something or other. I kept saying, 'No thank you, I'm not interested. No thank you.' He was so persistent, and my friend said, 'Go to dinner with him,' and eventually I agreed. We had Chinese food, my choice, and it turned out Bill doesn't like Chinese food and despite him not liking the meal, we had a really great time. I'd totally misjudged this person who I thought I had no interest in. We ended up moving to Frankfurt, got married in 1993 in Denmark and our daughter Madeline arrived shortly thereafter."

LTC Walters had interests similar to Edwards' at school, but his route into the Army differed: "I had a passion while I was at high school for football, similar to Bill, but when I finished my senior year, I knew I wasn't fast enough to go up to the next level. You had to be bigger and quicker. I was about 6 ft 2 and 200 lbs coming out of high school, but I just wasn't fast enough and couldn't jump high, or anything like that. I knew I wasn't going to compete at the collegiate level. I did receive a four-year reserve officers' training corps scholarship coming out of high school and went to the local college, Jacksonville State University, located in northern Alabama and that's where I started going to college.

"What I started doing in college as a hobby was scuba diving. That was a big passion. Me and a couple of buddies did our open water diving in northern Florida in a crystal clear, cold sinkhole. We would dive there to get used to our equipment, the various depths etc. Then we dived in the Gulf of Mexico.

"Then, during the summers, when I wasn't in college, I'd be down in Florida, because I had family there in a place called Amelia Island, just north of Jacksonville. I worked at a papermill down there, because both of my grandfathers had worked at this papermill. I was kind of a legacy now. There was no way they couldn't hire me for the summer!

"I had the worst job in the mill. The first summer, I was the 'janitor's assistant.' Anything the janitor didn't want to do, it was like, 'Hey Bob. I've got a job for you.' When I had time off, there was this one specific retired Navy chief and he loved to scuba dive but couldn't get his buddies to go with him all the time. This guy had a boat and a compressor in his shed where we could fill our tanks. We would spearfish and one guy would carry a bang stick, which is basically a pole which has a shotgun shell or a 357 Magnum shell at the end and you would bang it up against the side of a big fish and it detonates the charge, and that charge went right through that fish. But that was only for protection, because we would fish for big grouper or snapper and when you shot one of those with a speargun, they don't die straight away, and they are not very happy about getting shot with a speargun. As this fish is flopping around in the water and it's bleeding, that was a big attraction to sharks and that's when the bang stick came into play, as you were making your way up to the boat.

"Unlike Bill though, I dropped out of college and enlisted in the Army."

Joining the Army was more of a case of necessity for Walters and his childhood sweetheart: "Nancy and I met at high school in Kansas, in 1977. It was at the Leavenworth high school orientation, when they bring in all the new kids in the day before class starts, so we can know where our lockers are at, the classes, etc. Nancy was a sophomore, 10th grade, and I was a junior, 11th grade. That's when we started dating.

"Both Nancy and I were from military families. My dad was in the Army and her dad was in the United States Marine Corps. He was in charge of the marine detachment of the disciplinary barracks at Fort Leavenworth and the last thing Master Sergeant Peterson wanted, was for his oldest daughter to be dating the son of an Army officer. I started out at the very bottom of the family totem pole.

"Then what happened was, my father moved away from Leavenworth and we then all moved to Alabama. Nancy and I stayed in contact for about a year or so, then she dumped me. However, we re-established contact, got together again and got married at sunset on Valentine's Day, February 14, 1981, in Alabama, on Cheaha Mountain, which is the highest point in Alabama. It wasn't an elaborate wedding by any stretch. My mother and father came over from Germany, which is where my father was stationed at this point, and one of my friends did the photos with a little Instamatic camera.

"I was still in college and Nancy traveled down to Jacksonville State, Alabama, and then we found out a few months later during that summer that she was pregnant with our first child, Martina. We didn't have any health insurance so we went to the Blue Cross Blue Shield, which is a health insurance company in the States, which would insure college couples. When we explained that Nancy was pregnant, they said, 'That's a pre-existing medical condition, so we can't help with that one.' So, I went from there to the recruiting station and enlisted in the Army,

September 3, 1981. Martina is directly responsible for me joining the Army!

"I went off for basic training, while Nancy went back to her mom and dad in Kansas. I graduated from basic training in December and went back to Kansas. Martina was born on December 27, 1981, and my career progressed from there onwards.

Introduction

A Bad Vibe

You have to remember that Abu Ghraib was a prison, but also a forward operating base. It had a wall around it just like a penitentiary, but inside there were concrete buildings with prison wings. That's where the U.S. Army Reserve Military Police Brigade was, and they were in charge of the prison detainees. Then there were some disused textile production warehouses where the foundations of the looms were still in the concrete floors. This is where we, the 165th Military Intelligence Battalion, were set up.

The reserve unit that had occupied the area lacked military discipline and had not done any appreciable work to the security, or work to improve the living conditions of their soldiers. It was squalor. The discipline had completely broken down in that unit, so when we showed up in November 2003, they weren't saluting officers, they weren't properly dressed in military uniforms and were not maintaining their weapons. It was a mess. The sanitary conditions were poor, everything was dirty, and weapons were totally clogged with dust. It was very poor organization.

We were living in this facility and about a hundred meters away were thousands of Iraqi prisoners bunched in between a concertina wire fence. If they rioted or broke out, we were in the middle of it. It was a very tense situation.

Abu Ghraib was a place where you could not live outside of a concrete building, because you would die due to the number of mortars and rockets. You did not hang out in the open areas. We occupied the buildings we needed to occupy to make sure our soldiers were protected.

Overall, the place was very eerie. You were literally standing on

Top and bottom: Artwork of Saddam Hussein in a disused textile factory in Abu Ghraib. The artwork was painted by facility staff under Saddam's reign (Romeo Qureishi's collection).

the bones of dead Iraqis. So many people previously had been executed there during Saddam Hussein's regime. The whole place had a bad vibe and had a cemetery feel to it and that never went away along with the smell of the place.

—Mike Flentie, Assistant Operations Officer,
165th Military Intelligence Battalion

Prologue
Ambushed

DATE: December 3, 2003

LOCATION: ABU GHRAIB

That day in December was no different from any other day in Abu Ghraib prison, Iraq, inasmuch as the blueprint for normality didn't exist in the first place. However, this particular episode made worldwide headlines as those involved demonstrated another level of integrity, loyalty and pride at the drop of a hat.

Major Edwards explained the context leading up to December 3, 2003: "We'd been there for about a week. E Company, 51st Infantry Regiment were conducting combat operations every day. In fact, in the time we were in Iraq, the 165th Battalion, specifically E Company conducted over four hundred combat operations.

"This is how those operations worked. We would send out a long-range surveillance team in about three or four trucks with machine guns on top, with each truck holding four soldiers, which included a driver, a tactical commander and a gunner, who would be up there with a crew-served weapon. It's called 'crew-served,' because it requires two or more individuals to ensure it operates efficiently. Example of such weapons include the M60 and .50 caliber machine guns, anti-tank weapons or anti-aircraft guns.

"A team of three long-range surveillance soldiers would be the absolute minimum in each truck, but technically you'd have a fourth guy in the back to assist that gunner. The soldiers would then be inserted into a designated location in total darkness and would hide in the neighboring areas over a period of a day or two, sometimes even three.

"So, you have to imagine, the patrols are moving at night in blackout conditions, in the middle of the desert or suburbs of western Baghdad, depending on the mission. Think about how hard that is." LTC Walters added. "There was a place along the prison wall in Abu Ghraib where you could roll it back and slide these guys out, with minimal signature. If the enemy was surveying us entering the control point, we could slide these guys out the other entrance that we normally kept barricaded and they would be under blackout drive, which meant their headlights and lights inside the vehicle were all extinguished. They would then proceed using night-vision goggles while driving to the intended coordinates.

"On arrival, we'd do an insertion and drop off the team. They would then do an infiltration on foot to get to where their hide site would be and from there establish a surveillance site a short distance away to counter indirect fire. Normally they would put two soldiers up in the surveillance site, who were responsible for watching the area and identifying enemy personnel combat activities. The guys in the hide site would be responsible for establishing communications and planning activities.

"We did an analysis of the points of origin where insurgents set up their rockets and mortars and had fired a few rounds at the forward operating base and then broke everything down and drove away. Based on that analysis you'd map some reconnaissance looking at overhead imagery, to determine 'hide' locations, where we would insert the long-range surveillance team and they could conceal themselves. If the team were to see the enemy, they would shoot them or call for the artillery team.

"We did these combat operations routinely to try to mitigate some of the enemy's attacks on us over the current period of time and would coordinate with the other units in the area to improve the force protection at the operating base of Abu Ghraib."

Major Edwards added: "When it was time to exit, they would collapse the surveillance site and move any traces that they'd been there, relocate to the hide site then collapse that site and do an exfiltration to the extraction point, where another team would come in with, once again, three or four gun trucks, extract the long-range surveillance team and bring them back to the forward operating base. That's kind of how it played out.

"Back to December 3rd. Late that evening the patrol left Abu Ghraib in three vehicles. They were going to go roughly 17–20km south of the forward operating base from Baghdad to carry out a reconnaissance mission, to obtain information about the enemy. Everything seemed to be fine.

"At this time, I'm at the tactical operations center (TOC) around 10 p.m.–11 p.m. in the area near where I slept, watching an episode of the TV series *The Sopranos*. At this time it was late and most people were in their offices or sleeping areas. Then the radio started crackling with chatter, with MEDEVAC (evacuation of military casualties to hospital by vehicle or helicopter) calls coming in. I ran into Bob's room and said straight away, 'Something's going on in the TOC.' We got hold of the battalion operations officer and all went in there.

"Once we got everyone in together, the ops guys were taking charge of the long-range surveillance reports that were coming in. By now, the long-range surveillance guys who were on the ground were fighting and when you heard the radio, you could hear 50 caliber machine guns and various other weapons going off.

"An infantry specialist at the time and some of the guys who were on the patrol were calling in requesting MEDEVAC, because they were in contact with the enemy and had been ambushed. This specialist was about twenty years old and bearing in mind the pressure he was under at that point, incredibly, he wasn't screaming into the microphone. It was calm, controlled and methodical communication."

Prior to hearing his voice on the radio, Major Edwards had not crossed paths with the soldier, but LTC Walters had experienced occasional interaction with the young infantry specialist: "He had been with long-range surveillance the entire time, participating in surveillance missions up at the camp in Balad, which was a little north of Baghdad. We were doing counter indirect fire surveillance missions and he was on duty with other soldiers at the entry control point.

"My direct access with him was limited, due to the several echelons of command between us. He was junior enlisted, had a squad leader, a platoon sergeant, a platoon leader, a first sergeant, and a company commander between us. However, by this stage we'd been deployed for ten months or so and you get to know your soldiers, simply because, when you are doing your battlefield circulation, popping into the entry control point, or taking a briefing from a team that's about to be inserted. So, I had intermittent conversations with him prior to that night, enough to recognize his voice when he gave the report over the radio."

Edwards recounted the memorable moment when challenge in the face of adversity became a life or death situation: "We had a platoon from the 82nd Airborne Division living with us on Abu Ghraib. At any given time you're going to have transient folks coming through and bedding down on the forward operating base just to provide them with some security and rest prior to them continuing with their mission. The 82nd was attached to our battalion for a set period of time but would be replaced. They were there to help provide security, mortar fire and quick reaction force capability and this was one of those occasions where all that came together in one episode.

"It was the middle of the night and I ran into the living quarters and shouted to the platoon sergeant of the 82nd, 'The long-range surveillance team is under attack. We need a quick reaction force team straight away. Can you guys roll?' He was sitting on his cot that he slept on and yelled into this dark warehouse where all these soldiers were asleep, 'You guys get your asses up! Long-range surveillance is in trouble, we need to get moving.'

"They were sleeping with their weapons and ammunition and rose instantly. They assembled their trucks in a really short time period and we gave them a grid coordinate of where the ambush was taking place. Next thing they were rolling out the gate going out from Abu Ghraib to help and support these guys. For me it was one of those amazing moments and since that time, I've been so proud to have been an American officer seeing this take form during combat operations.

"The ops team in the tactical operations center was now supporting the MEDEVAC operation and the specialist. By this stage he and his team was under fire and heavily outnumbered by thirty-five enemy insurgents, resulting in hits from three RPGs (rocket propelled grenades), three IEDs (Improvised Explosive Devices), and gun fire."

Walters added: "In addition to everything happening in the middle of the night, detainee operations were still occurring in Abu Ghraib. We still had several thousand detainees inside the fenced area in tents and high value detainees and interrogations were happening in the constructed jail or hard sites.

"That particular night, when I was alerted to the troops in contact, I was at the tactical operations center listening to the radio. The long-range surveillance and insertion teams were dropped off and the guys in the trucks were returning to the forward operating base. That's when an RPG came in and hit the right front tire of one of our vehicles— the vehicle the specialist was in. That particular round tore up the leg of the sergeant sitting up front that was in charge of that vehicle and it also disabled the truck. That sergeant would later go on to die from those injuries several months later.

"When you're under fire, you return fire. During an ambush you have your weapons systems set up so that there's an ideal area that you can maximize the effects of fire on your target. Our guys were in the middle of that kill zone and they had to push the disabled vehicle out. In the left front seat was the driver, standing in the center of the vehicle was the gunner, the specialist was in the back seat and his sergeant, his boss, was screaming in pain because he'd just had his leg ripped apart from an RPG round.

"The specialist's fellow soldier had a 50 caliber crew-served weapon and knowing this could be the key to winning the exchange of fire, he placed himself in front of the gunner, in essence turning himself into a shield. At this point, the specialist's unit started to gain the upper hand on the enemy.

"Despite sustaining injuries to his chest and arms through two gunshots and eleven pieces of shrapnel, he continued to lead and secure a defensive perimeter and relayed information to headquarters about the enemy's position. He would eventually be awarded the Silver Star for gallantry in action and recognized by President George W. Bush during a State of the Union address. However, at this point I had no idea that he'd been injured.

"As the driver was trying to keep the vehicle straight and get out of the kill zone, the specialist came up on the radio and started providing the situation report of the troops in contact and the request for the MEDEVAC.

"At this point, the quick reaction force team were rolling out the requirement for MEDEVAC and everything else. That's all happening during this thirty to forty-five minutes of high activity level in our tactical operations center. I then get a report from the long-range surveillance company commander and he's running down the list of wounded from the attack and one of the names on it was the specialist. I said, 'That's not possible because I heard him on the radio.' He said, 'Sir. He's been hit and he's being MEDEVACed to the combat Army surgical hospital.'"

Major Edwards added: "Carrying on from Bob. I'm talking to the 82nd quick reaction force guys and they're rolling out with only a grid coordinate. Remember, it's the middle of the night, they're just waking up, but their adrenaline was working overtime. I remember running out before they left and they had loaded between six and eight soldiers on open Humvees, with soldiers facing outwards all along the beds of the trucks, packing a lot of firepower.

"They got to the long-range surveillance location of the ambush in about twenty minutes. Absolutely amazing. I ran into the tactical operations center and talked to Bob and the other officers. 'Hey. The quick reaction force is rolling. I'm going to go up and alert the maintenance guys to get ready for recovery of the vehicles.' In essence, towing the damaged vehicles back to the forward operating base with tow straps.

"Once the 82nd guys reached the objective, MEDEVAC and extraction was beginning to take place, and they were also fighting off the remnants of that enemy. They walked into a fight and were making sure there was no enemy left before gathering all of the equipment and trucks, in order to tow them back to base. The actions of the quick reaction force on arrival might seem partly reactive, but if your unit's trained, you can do these things when bad things happen. That's how I always viewed it.

"I ran up to the maintenance section of Abu Ghraib in LSA (Life Support Area) Mustang, found the battalion maintenance officer and explained that the vehicles needed to be brought back. He replied, 'Roger that, sir.' By now the quick reaction force from the 82nd had now cleared the objective and were bringing the equipment back. Bob and I inherently knew what we thought we were going to see, which were vehicles that were destroyed by RPGs, machine gun fire and evidence of physical injury. What we didn't want to do was bring those vehicles back and let all of our soldiers see the damage and all the things that were bad about that situation. We wanted to take care of that in the middle of the night. Get the vehicles cleaned, prepared and repaired.

"I remember the guys from the 82nd bringing the truck back to the maintenance area which the specialist and his fellow sergeant who had been hit in the leg by the RPG were in. The whole right front of the truck had been blown away. I couldn't believe how much damage the RPG had done. In that ambush, there was not a soldier who was involved who was not wounded that night. We have to give credit to the MEDEVAC operations, the helicopter crews, who reacted very quickly and got the guys to the combat support hospitals.

"The inside of the truck told another story. There was a bunch of brass (empty shell cases) laying around in the truck from the guys firing back at the enemy. But more memorable and brutal was the amount of blood and pieces of flesh scattered around. One of the rifles was still in the truck and was completely covered in blood. I ran it over to the medical station and got some alcohol and cleaned the weapon. I didn't want to give it back to the company looking like that."

Walters recalled: "Wounded soldiers had been transported by helicopter from a landing zone just outside where the ambush took place, over to the hospital for further treatment. This particular vehicle that was coming back in—we had a responsibility as leaders to minimize the psychological impact to our soldiers. We washed down the truck as best as we could within five or ten minutes, then we turned the vehicle over to the mechanics to start repairing as best as they could.

"When they came back that night we immediately did an after action report at about 2am. This episode was over, but the next one was always a heartbeat away. At Abu Ghraib prison, we were constantly under the stress of being mortared, rocketed and attacked under gunfire. It was 24/7 and the dented walls surrounding the prison reflected that. Even simple tasks like getting up in the morning and walking over to the mess hall to get a cup of coffee or something to eat, you were exposing yourself to the unknown, because the place was so volatile. I would put my flak vest on, my helmet and everything just to walk to the bathroom.

"Everyone who has ever served at Abu Ghraib prison has a story. This is ours."

1

The Day That Changed the World

"U.S. Attacked

Hijacked jets destroy twin towers and hit pentagon in day of terror."
—*New York Times* front page, September 12, 2001

It was possibly America's darkest day. Irrespective of which country you were in, if you were old enough to remember, you'll never forget the exact moment you got wind of the terrorist attacks on September 11, 2001. For anybody serving in the U.S. Army, that memory was far more poignant.

A group of nineteen Islamic extremists, under the banner of Al-Qaeda, hijacked four passenger airplanes to undertake the most memorable suicide mission in the United States history. At 8.45 a.m. on September 11, a Boeing 767 aircraft crashed into the north tower of the iconic twin towers, in the financial district of Lower Manhattan. Eighteen minutes later, a second 767 crashed into the south tower, then at 9.45 a.m. another aircraft plowed into the west side of the Pentagon, killing 125 personnel.

Twenty-five minutes later, the fourth and final vessel hurled into a field at full speed in Pennsylvania, after the passengers on board heroically took on their hijackers. Fatalities on board all four planes totaled more than 260, including the terrorists; however, in the next twenty minutes, the twin towers collapsed, killing over 2,600 in the buildings and surrounding area. The attack took almost 3,000 innocent souls in less than two hours.

Major Edwards cast his mind back to the day when Al-Qaeda turned jet planes into bombs, killing thousands and raising the bar for global terrorism: "I was an instructor at the University of Tennessee in Knoxville, training reserve Army training corps cadets when 9/11 happened. I was with ten cadets in our team room getting ready for classes and we were watching this really old TV that still had the turn dials on it, most likely something that had been donated. Suddenly, breaking news flashed up on the screen. 'Terrorists attack New York, Pentagon.'

"There we were watching the planes hit the World Trade Center and I turned around to the guys I was standing with and said, 'Your lives have just changed.' They replied straight away, 'What are you talking about? What do you mean?' I said, 'I will guarantee you that we will be going to one of these really distant places very soon, based on this attack on the homeland.'

"Fast forward to 2003 and four of those ten had been commissioned, which means they were made second lieutenants in the Army and were in Iraq the same time Bob and I were there for Operation Iraqi Freedom 1. They were platoon leaders in infantry and transportation units and two of those guys were in Balad, Iraq, the same time we were at the 165th. At some point I got to sit down and have lunch with them and see how their jobs were going. When I did see them, they said, 'You were absolutely right that day at the University of Tennessee. It did change our lives.' Within weeks of 9/11 happening, the U.S. Army was in Afghanistan, then we went into Iraq in 2003.

"At that point of my career, I'd been in the Army nearly fourteen years and been deployed to the Middle East at least four times before 9/11. I was an Armor battalion headquarters and headquarters company commander and brigade and battalion intelligence officer and we were doing what was called 'intrinsic action' deployments to Kuwait. We were going out there sending a battalion to the desert to train soldiers, plus add a show of force and support for the Kuwaitis. I did this multiple times, so for me, my deployments to the Middle East started before 9/11. I was very familiar with Camp Doha in Kuwait. After it happened, the pace and the strain of the deployments was fast and furious, and on the families it was the unknown of when you were going and coming back."

LTC Walters added: "Just to differentiate between combat deployments and non-combat deployments. Prior to 9/11, I only had one combat deployment, which was Operation Desert Shield (the codename for the Gulf War 1990–91) and Desert Storm as the company commander stationed at Fort Bragg."

On February 28, 1991, a ceasefire was negotiated between the UN coalition and Iraq, which led to the hostilities of the Gulf War being sus-pended. Twelve years later and the U.S. Army was putting a great deal of time and resources into removing Saddam Hussein from the picture as a result of the brutal atrocities and genocide he had been responsible for. Abu Ghraib was a case in point. To an extent, 9/11 acted as the added springboard of motivation to fully engage with the Iraqi Invasion, with Bush formally announcing a "War on Terror." The first chapter of a pro-tracted conflict which began in March 2003 was named Operation Iraqi Freedom 1.

LTC Walters continued: "After 9/11, I've had six combat deploy-ments in total. Two in Iraq and four in Afghanistan. My second com-bat deployment was as a battalion commander during Operation Iraqi Freedom 1 as a lieutenant colonel, based out of Germany with V Corps. After that it was in Afghanistan as a squadron commander in a joint spe-cial operations taskforce. Back as a brigade commander in Iraq out of Fort Hood and then back in Afghanistan twice as the senior intelligence officer, another special operations taskforce. Fourth one in Afghani-stan, which was my most recent one (2016–17), as a senior intel offi-cer for Operation Resolute Support and Freedom's Sentinel, which were the two missions we had going on there. Resolute Support was a train, advise and assist mission. There was also Operation Inherent Resolve which was basically our counter terrorism mission against ISIS in Iraq.

"As far as regular deployments, prior to 9/11, I'd been stationed in Germany, Korea and Colombia. Each of the Colombia deployments were about four to five months. Since 9/11, I haven't done routine type deployments. They've all been combat. That one event in 2001 impacted our future deployments without a doubt."

One thing many civilians forget about soldiers is that they have a life outside of the military, irrespective of what type of deployment they are assigned to. That harsh reality of that life can rear its head in the most untimely and devastating ways at any given moment, as Walters was about to find out.

2

The Other Theater

"Trust in God with all your heart."—Proverbs 3:5–6

Early March 2003, under the banner of Operation Iraqi Freedom I, the U.S. was getting ready to lead a coalition to overthrow Saddam Hussein. According to *Socialist Worker Online*, "The French political scientist Dominique Reynié estimated that, between 3 January and 12 April 2003, some 36 million people took part in nearly 3,000 protests around the world against the Iraq war in over 800 cities."

Major Edwards expressed his stance: "For me, I didn't pay any attention to that, because 9/11 had happened and we were already engaged in Afghanistan and were now engaged in Iraq. It was Charlie Mike (continue mission). That was white noise for me."

LTC Walters added: "I agree with Bill one hundred percent. The only concern that I had was leaving my wife and children, because they were in Germany. There's very little you can do to affect things back at home once you take off."

While Walters was en route to Iraq, his wife, Nancy, and two daughters, Daytona and Martina, were back at the U.S. military base in Darmstadt, Germany, which was not an ideal location to be at that moment in time. Nancy explained: "Between Bob's deployment and living in a country that did not support the U.S.'s involvement in Iraq, that was extreme. The Germans did not just protest but were burning fences at the entrance to the base in Darmstadt, threatening Americans and the families of soldiers."

The disdain from the host nation against American soldiers was hostile, yet manageable. However, when their daughter was taken ill, concern was ramped up several levels. Daytona recalled: "I was seventeen at the time and started passing out in class as a result of a heart condition called Prolonged QT Interval. On March 19, 2003 as the war on Iraq was declared, I ended up being admitted to a local German hospital in Wiesbaden, Germany. They couldn't fly me back to the States commercially because the risk was too high and the military airlift was prioritized to the war.

"My mom and sister all have the same condition, so at the hospital, they said, based on family history the best thing would be to put in an ICD (implantable cardio-defibrillator), however, I had to wait eight days before they could do the procedure. They admitted me to the hospital and wouldn't let me leave because my heart was too unstable.

"Germany was against the U.S.' decision to go to war in Iraq and since I was the daughter to a senior U.S. soldier going out there, I didn't get the warmest reception. My mom stayed with me at the hospital while people spat on the floor and said horrible things about being an American and that we should be ashamed of our president and things like that. Me and my mom did our best to distract from the situation by playing Yahtzee and card games. It was like an odd little bubble of happiness in a really unfortunate situation."

When you're in a hostile situation, you must look for solace and comfort. For Daytona, that came in the form of her Christian faith, which she leaned on heavily through this next horrific episode: "The night before my surgery, my prayer was for peace. I was anxious. The combination of my Papa not being there, the operation and the negativity from the Germans turned it into a really bad week. Although I hadn't been able to speak live to Papa in a bit, he called my hospital room the night before my surgery to tell me he was praying for me.

"My mom had the same surgery a few months prior, so I had an idea of how it would go, but I was really struggling with the anxiety of that. What I hadn't banked on was them performing the procedure without anesthesia, which didn't seem real at first. I started kicking and screaming and trying to fight, but you're strapped in during surgery so you don't roll off. Instead, they laid two nurses over my legs so they could continue the procedure. The surgeon was having trouble placing the lead into my heart and decided to pull them out aggressively. I started singing the song, 'God of Wonders,' louder and louder and they started yelling at me to shut up. The procedure lasted a little over two and a half hours.

"The second part of my prayer was about midway through the surgery where I asked God to let me die. I didn't understand the amount of hate I was being exposed to as I'd never met these people before. The pain was sublime. More than I could wrap my head around.

23

"After the surgery, on the way to recovery I saw my mom and started screaming, explaining to her everything that had happened. She immediately found someone to get me some pain medicine which was great."

Nancy recalled the nightmare in vivid color from the outset: "The day she was admitted to the hospital was the same day that the news was broadcasting on German television that the United States was engaged in battle in Iraq. That was on TV in this German hospital. On that day, we had doctors and translators, but the doctor thankfully spoke English very well. Daytona emphasized over and over again, 'Well, I don't care about these details, because I'll be asleep, right?' The doctor said, 'Of course you'll be asleep.' On the day of the surgery I shook his hand for taking care of my daughter. He had two daughters, so I assumed he would have empathy with my daughter. Or so I thought. They said it would be roughly two and a half hours, but I knew that could mean three, possibly four.

"I sat there and at some point after two hours, I wanted an update. I went up to the reception and asked the lady there. I even asked in German and she just said, 'You Americans,' and slammed the glass screen in front of my face. I started running up to different people asking them for an update. None of the Germans wanted to help.

"There was a French nun who heard me and could now see I was getting a little frantic. She said, 'I'll find out what the update is on your daughter for you.' In the meantime, one of the nurses, who had been in with Daytona walked out. I walked up to her and said, 'Are you guys finished? How's Daytona? Where do I go next?' She looked at me, said, 'You Americans,' spat in front of me, pulled out a cigarette and walked outside.

"The nun comes back out and says, 'They've finished the surgery and your daughter has been taken to ICU.' I took off with Martina somewhere behind me trying to find where this was. I was talking to the lady at the ICU desk and she said they would come out of this particular elevator. So, I'm standing at this elevator waiting and in the distance I start to hear screaming like a wild animal type of screaming. It wasn't coming from this elevator, it was coming from a different one, where they brought up cargo.

"I went running over because I knew it was Daytona's scream and ran around to the elevator, banging on the button. When the doors opened, the medical technicians who were at the head and the foot of her bed, were both crying. The one closest to me said, 'Don't judge Germany by this.'

"Daytona was wide awake. We had made jokes before the operation how we would put things in her mouth when she was out cold, but her nightmare of being awake in any form came true in its worst form. She was screaming for help and didn't know who I was. When I finally grabbed her face and told her who I was, she said, 'They hurt me and wouldn't make me go to sleep Mama. They kept me awake.' I'm holding her hand as she was put into this ICU room. I could barely feel my legs. I grabbed the nurse and said, 'Knock her out, now.' She started to pretend that she didn't understand English. I grabbed her and repeated myself, 'Knock her out.' She understood this time and gave Daytona pain medication to allow her to sleep.

"I then slid down the wall and put my head between my legs. I didn't know what was happening and had no way to contact Bob, because the war had started and I knew he was in the fight. I just didn't know how I was going to move forward. At one point I ran out and the brigade commander's wife was there and I told her what happened. We then had military posted for the rest of our stay at the hospital while Daytona recovered from the surgery and became stable. Which felt like eternity."

Daytona continued to recall her horrendous experience: "The third part of my prayer that night was that I'd forget everything that had happened. I had to stay in at the hospital after the surgery for a number of days, but before I left, I had the opportunity to confront the surgeon. On seeing him, my first reaction was panic. I protected the side of my body where the surgery had occurred, then I calmed down enough to ask him, 'Why did you do it?' He responded with, 'Next time, kick and scream in German.' Then he got up and left the room. To be faced with that kind of evil was hard to understand.

"I stayed in the hospital for a few more days, which brought the total stay to about eleven or twelve days, went home and went into a really dark place for a long time. I ended up being diagnosed with PTSD (post-traumatic stress disorder), depression, anxiety and would often have flashbacks and night terrors. I started going to counseling, but also taking antidepressants and sleep aids. Since they were prescribed 'as needed,' I'd take them as and when I wanted, which as an insecure seventeen-year-old in trauma, with a scar on her chest wasn't a great thing.

"I got to a place where it felt like too much in my head. I

contemplated suicide, by taking an overdose, but the Lord reminded me of my mom. Killing myself would have been selfish and my mom would have blamed herself. I couldn't do that."

Nancy also admitted, "After what happened to Daytona, I was diagnosed with PTSD and for a while spoke with a counselor as I tried to process and get my head around it all."

Daytona graduated high school in 2003, returned to the States and moved in with her grandparents in Kansas: "For my first semester at school I was working as a technology assistant for a school district and was going to school full time at night. By now, I'd gotten addicted to the pain medicines.

"Back in the day of instant messenger, I'd sent a message to my mom in Germany, because I thought I was meeting her, but I'd written gibberish, because of the medication. That was a bad day. She got in touch with my grandpa to come and pick me up at work. When he came and got me, he asked for my purse and emptied it all out and said, 'You've got to get through this.' He got rid of the tablets and the next few days were awful. Physically I needed to navigate through the withdrawal symptoms. For the first time I had to face everything I was feeling which the medicine had numbed. It was a very awful seventy-two hours and I was very mean to them. Little by little I got through it.

"We got to a place where both me and my mom were able to pray for forgiveness for the surgeon, which in all honesty is not what I wanted to do at first. I ended up moving back to Germany at the end of 2003 to be with my mom, because my dad was still deployed and my sister moved back to the States."

Sister Martina added: "We still had to live our lives. It was another step in the process, but it wasn't easy. There were no group talking platforms like we have now. I would get updates from mom, grandma and grandpa. When Daytona was struggling, I would dream about her, then call her and tell her, 'Today is a new day. You need to keep on keeping on and you will overcome this.' We weren't speaking frequently, and I'd have dreams that she wanted to end her life and I'd immediately get out of bed and drop to my knees and pray for her. It was tough."

Daytona's ordeal was incredibly stressful for Nancy, but unfortunately, it was not her only concern at this point. As the wife of a deployed battalion commander, with the U.S. at war, Nancy's duties went beyond that of a wife and a mother: "While I was with Daytona in the hospital, Martina was dealing with the threats at the house in Darmstadt, which was an hour away. The military police had come to let her know, that the name plates which had the soldier's name and rank had to come off the front doors of all the houses at the post and the American flag had to be taken down, to make it as sterile as possible, so as not to be identified as a target.

"Instead of sending out emails to the families about fun places to go and visit, we had to now tell them where they could not go because of active threats and protests. The literature and counselling were not fully in place yet and we had no idea how long our soldiers would be gone. It was an incredibly volatile time."

Daytona continued: "Surgery was on March 27, 2003 and on the anniversary, I would drink a lot and say really awful things about anything to do with Germany. I'm embarrassed to think about what I said, but at the time I was emotionally wounded. Little by little I stopped getting drunk and saying awful things about the German people."

Daytona's surgery wasn't in vain. After sharing her story with various groups, she has inspired many others to come to terms with what life can sometimes harshly present them. Perhaps more importantly, she's also got herself back on a path of liberation: "In 2015 I was flying out to Kansas for my sister's wedding, which I was very excited about. On March 28th I woke up and felt like I'd forgotten to do something. I was looking at my maid of honor's to-do list and everything was taken care of, but then it hit me. March 27 came and went. Finally, twelve years after the surgery I'd forgotten about the date. That was part of the prayer that was answered."

Since her operation in 2003, Daytona has had two further ICD replacement surgeries in the U.S. The surgeon who conducted the procedures said, "It was a terrible mess in there."

Daytona agreed: "It really was. On so many levels."

3

When Bill Met Bob

"Important encounters are planned by the souls, long before the bodies see each other."—Paulo Coelho

On March 22, 2003, President George W. Bush addressed the United States over the radio:

> In this war, our coalition is broad, more than forty countries from across the globe. Our cause is just, the security of the nations we serve and the peace of the world. And our mission is to clear, to disarm Iraq of weapons of mass destruction, to end Saddam Hussein's support of terrorism, and to free the Iraqi people.

Between March 19, 2003, and May 1, 2003, a U.S. led coalition composed of almost 180,000 troops invaded Iraq. Approximately 130,000 soldiers were from the U.S. and around 45,000 from the United Kingdom. On March 20 there was an airstrike on the presidential palace in Baghdad and the day after the coalition launched an attack into Basra Province.

LTC Walters recalled his engagement with other countries from the coalition: "Little to none. You might have forty countries in the collation, but you might only have one person from that country to represent that statistic. We kept the brigade informed of our specific mission which was our principal focus. As far as coordinating with other members of the coalition, it wasn't required at battalion level. We had our own infrastructure within the U.S. Army, in the same way the coalition guys had their own missions. The end goal was similar, but our unit missions differed."

From the turn of the 1960s up to the early 1990s, Iraq had invested a great deal of resources into researching the various forms of weapons of mass destruction and their potency. Towards the latter half of that timeframe, they put theory into practice and not only produced the weapons, but unfortunately also implemented them to deadly effect. Iraq's president, Saddam Hussein was globally chastised for his barbaric use of chemical weapons during his conflict with Iran in the 1980s, but by the early '90s it seemed a corner might have been turned.

After the Persian War, the United Nations, alongside the Iraqi government, found and destroyed large stockpiles of chemical weapons, amongst other equipment and munitions. However, by the early 2000s, both George W. Bush and the U.K.'s prime minister, Tony Blair, had a strong belief that not only did Iraq still possess weapons of mass destruction, but that they were actively manufacturing them.

Walters commented: "When we were in Germany and the initial planning was happening, there were intelligence officers looking to identify potential sites of where the weapons of mass destruction might be at. I personally never saw any intel that pointed towards anything. Now, I wasn't a planner at the corps level, so I didn't see everything those guys saw, but I sat through several briefings, and we did major rehearsals prior to deploying down to Kuwait. I saw a lot of the classified material that was in play, where senior decision makers were making decisions, but I personally never saw anything that had anything to do with weapons of mass destruction."

Major Edwards added, "I didn't see anything either, but I don't think we would have been privy to that type of information if it had been available, just based on where we were at and what we were doing as a unit and our organizational mission."

One micro coalition that occurred as a result of Operation Iraqi Freedom 1 was between two soldiers who would go on to forge a lifetime friendship. Prior to 2003, Edwards and Walters had not crossed paths. Walters explained the journey that led him to command the 165th Military Intelligence Battalion in Abu Ghraib: "In 1990, I was a company commander in Fort Bragg, North Carolina. I'd just returned from a year in Korea as an intelligence officer for a tank battalion and then picked up my daughters Daytona, Martina and my wife Nancy who had been staying with my mom and dad down in Florida. I took a week's leave, went up to Fort Bragg, signed in, went to airborne refresher training which is like three days of jumping out of towers to get you prepared for airborne operations. The day I finished my training, I was returning to the 519th Military Intelligence Battalion area, which was a part of the 525th.

"The day I returned to the battalion area, there was all kinds of activity going on. I was thinking, 'This is exactly why I wanted to be at

Fort Bragg, because there was always something exciting happening.' As I'm going up the stairs to see the battalion operations officer, down came the battalion commander. I was a brand-new captain, so I put my back up against the wall to make room for him, hoping he'd pass right by me. He stops right in front of me, looks down at my name tag and says, 'Walters. Are you ready to take command?' and I said 'Yes, sir.' 'You know what's going on today?' and I said, 'No, sir.' He said, 'Are you read-on yet?' Essentially, that meant that you read a document that stated the seriousness of protecting classified material, then you signed a non-disclosure agreement promising to protect the material. I replied, 'No, sir.' He said, 'Get over to corps and get read-on.' 'Yes, sir' and he goes marching off.

"I ran upstairs to the battalion operations officer, and he was just rolling around laughing. I said, 'What's going on sir?' and he said laughing, 'Walters, you don't know how lucky you are. Saddam Hussein has invaded Kuwait, we are going to war and the Charlie company commander just got relieved and you're the only captain without a job.' The very next day we deployed to Saudi Arabia for the Gulf War.

"When I got to my command in June of 2002 in Germany, at that point the 165th had a human intelligence platoon deployed in Kosovo. We were rotating human intelligence soldiers down there to sustain the support with the operation. Shortly after I got there and took command, I made a trip along with the command sergeant major to visit the troops we had down in Camp Bondsteel.

"We knew at that time that we were preparing for a possible deployment to Kuwait to go into Iraq, but we didn't have any firm timelines. We did the command visit and returned back to Germany and that's when we started preparing fairly quickly for a deployment to Kuwait and then on to Iraq."

Major Edwards recalled the 2003 deployment, including a rather eventful first day in Iraq. "I joined Bob's battalion in June of 2003 and here's how it happened. I was at Fort Leavenworth at the United States Command and General Staff College around March 2003, when we were told, 'You may get pulled out of school early, before graduation. There are unit slots which need to be filled.' Everybody was on this rollercoaster of 'What are we doing? Where are we going?' Initially, it was looking like I would be assigned as a brigade intelligence officer in a brigade combat team, then I got orders over email that I was going to go to the 205th Military Intelligence Brigade to be the Brigade Adjutant. I was really disappointed as I wanted to be either a brigade combat team intelligence officer, an executive officer, or an operations officer of a tactical military intelligence unit.

"So, we're now doing all the preparations with the families, and our cars and household goods have been shipped. We're sitting in a hotel outside of Kansas City airport and I get an email a day or two before we're supposed to fly to Germany, saying I'd been reassigned as the executive officer for the 165th. That was great luck and timing on my part, to drop into, in my opinion the best battalion in that brigade, and to be the executive officer was an honor. That was career changing for me.

"I then went directly to Germany a few days later and got my family into an apartment in a city called Langen which was outside of Rhein-Main airbase, near Frankfurt. It was a quick turnaround. My wife and daughters didn't end up getting all the furniture, clothes, etc. due to the shipment being lost in transit, so they ended up camping out in this German apartment for about four months until the Army transportation system located and delivered our property.

"I left Germany on a C17 aircraft which hadn't been rigged up with seats, so we had to lay on the cargo pallets and it was freezing cold. I didn't sleep much and the first thing that hit you after landing was the intense heat as there was no air conditioning at Baghdad International Airport (formerly Saddam International Airport. Changed name in April 2003 after the invasion.).

"I got to Baghdad International Airport and at the time the Army had set up a small reception area in a tent city. There was no phone book, so I was asking anyone in the area if they knew how I could reach the 165th. It was just by luck that a soldier knew who I was looking for. 'Do you know where the 165th are?' and he said, 'Yeah. I think they're in Balad.' I found the Army 1035 field phone and dialed a number that hit the communications node and transferred me to the tactical operations center in Balad. In chaos, luck is really important.

"I got on the field phone, got through to the tactical operations center and I think it was the operations sergeant major who took the call. I said, 'I'm in the country. I need a ride from Baghdad.' They got the long-range surveillance guys together and sent them down from Balad to pick me up. This action in itself generated a combat patrol for the guys coming down to get me, so I was grateful.

"There was also a young soldier travelling with me from Germany into Iraq who was a replacement for the long-range surveillance company. We got picked up then we swung over to V Corps headquarters at Camp Victory, Baghdad, to pick up Major Mickie Williams, who was the 205th brigade operations officer and was running the 205th tactical operations center. Prior to his deployment at that time, Mickie had managed majors in the human resource command. In theory, his first encounter with us was managing our files, but this was the first time I'd met him in person.

"Camp Victory was an interesting place. Prior to Operation Iraqi Freedom 1 it had been ransacked by the Iraqis, then in April 2003 we moved our soldiers in there and it would eventually have well in excess of 10,000 soldiers on site. The camp was named after V Corps, or Victory Corps, from Heidelberg, Germany and was occupied by the U.S. Army from April 2003. On site was the Al-Faw Palace, which Saddam Hussein had built in the 1990s, but we just referred to it as 'The Palace.'

"The first time I went there was when we picked up Mickie. We purely went into the headquarters, met Mickey and some of the other people and then we left. When I went down a few weeks later, I was going to meet with one of our sister battalions and went into the main palace, which was a bit surreal as the soldiers of the V Corps were now living there. The palace was surrounded by individual houses that were used by Saddam's inner circle to visit or stay. In those houses is where the V Corps headquarters had set up its operations, then later on they moved the headquarters into the palace itself.

"If you can envision walking into this grand palace and there were hundreds of soldiers with hundreds of cots, laundry hanging everywhere, rifles on display. There was still some of the palace furniture at the entrance and I remember sitting there on one of the couches and there was a DSN (Defense Switched Network) phone that allowed soldiers to call back to the U.S. or Germany. There were also swimming pools which weren't functioning. Later on, some unit figured out a way to fill one of them and use it, but I didn't get a chance to partake. Lastly, there was this couch in the palace that was left after the looting that soldiers would have their picture taken on. I did the same, but the picture is lost. When I went back in 2010, it had been completely renovated back to its grandeur. Beautiful chandeliers and marble everywhere. But when I was there in 2003, it was a different story.

"Back to the ride to Balad. I didn't have my weapon because it was at the tactical operations center. There was a young sergeant who I think was the non-commissioned officer in the lead or third vehicle and he says, 'Hey, Sir. Do you have a weapon?' I said, 'No. It's back in Balad.' He

Romeo at Saddam Hussein's Al-Faw Palace (Romeo Qureishi's collection).

shook his head and said, 'Shit. Okay. Take my 9mm pistol and I'll jump up on the 50 caliber, and here's some ammo in case anything happens on the way to Balad. You do know how to shoot a 9mm?' I said 'Yes, of course!' He was just giving me a hard time. I knew I would like the unit from that moment on.

"Camp Victory is where the corps headquarters was, and we were only there for about thirty or forty minutes. Mickie was doing some business there, so we picked him up and then we started on our way up to Balad driving north up the Main Supply Route, Tampa. I believe the actual name was Highway One, but we called it Main Supply Route, Tampa—even though, it was referred to by many as IED or Ambush Alley, because it was a gauntlet of a road.

"On the way we ran into what might have been an ambush, but certainly an engagement of some kind. A truck coming down from the southside of the highway opened fire on our movement. The guys in the first truck did exactly what they were supposed to and returned fire. I didn't really know what was happening because of the placement of the vehicle I was in until someone popped up on the radio and said, 'We're in contact.' We started doing battle drills where the trucks herringboned off the road and then the soldiers on the 50 caliber started firing back.

"It all happened really quick and nobody was hurt. I remember getting out of the Humvee I was in, and I had this 9mm pistol, a couple of magazines of ammo and I was standing in the middle of this highway, when one of the sergeants says, 'Sir, can you keep the traffic stopped?' So, there I am standing in the middle of this highway and I'm holding Iraqi traffic, not letting them go past our vehicles. I remember looking into the very first car where I'm stopping the traffic and there's this man and his family and they're just staring at me with a fearful look, almost saying, 'What the hell is going on here?' I'll never forget their faces. All I was trying to do was get to the 165th and this whole surreal event was going on. This was my first few hours in Iraq and a solid reminder of what was to come.

"We get going again on the road and pulled up to Balad. As I got into the battalion area, where the tactical operations center was set up, the ops sergeant major comes running out welcoming me to the unit.

"After the journey I had, I was extremely exhausted after not sleeping for 24 hours and it was very hot. So, I get to the tactical operations center and I met Bob for the first time and the first thing he says to me was, 'I hear you guys were in a little contact on the way up. Welcome to Iraq!' I said, 'Thank you, sir. I'd like to go and shave.' He said, 'Good idea and then we'll get you up to speed on what we're doing.' That was my first day getting to the 165th Battalion."

In addition to Iraqi soldiers, it soon became apparent that the U.S. military had other enemies, including certain nondescript spies. The landscape of post-conflict was taking shape in the summer of 2003.

4

Who Let the Dogs Out?

"To his dog, every man is Napoleon; hence the constant popularity of dogs."—Aldous Huxley

In addition to fighting the local insurgents in and around Baghdad, the U.S. Army was also up against man's best friend. LTC Walters explained: "Around late March, early April 2003, we had the task to provide surveillance of Objective Rams, an area which was located outside of Najaf, Iraq (to the west). It was the corps' initial objective during the first phase of the attack into Iraq from Kuwait. The location was south of Baghdad and the thought was to secure the location and give combat forces an opportunity to rearm and refuel prior to attacking Baghdad.

"We inserted three, six-man long-range surveillance teams 800km into Iraq from Kuwait on a CH-47 Chinook aircraft, to provide eyes on surveillance and situational awareness for the lead unit, the 3rd Infantry Division.

"We did some false insertions at night where the Chinooks would land just for a few seconds, then fly off and land somewhere else, then take off again, so that any Iraqi soldiers who were observing these aircrafts would not know exactly what was happening. To their knowledge, soldiers were being dropped at these points, but if it was a false insertion point, no U.S. soldiers would be present.

"Two of the teams got into their hide sites and quickly constructed subsurface surveillance positions adjacent to them where they could see Objective Rams and then they reported in. The third team, upon insertion had their position compromised when some Bedouin farmers dogs started barking at them. The farmers then responded to the dogs, which led to the farmers letting the Iraqis know that there were Americans on the ground there.

"That long-range surveillance team consequently had to break contact for 48 hours to evade attack. After the dogs followed the team to their secondary site, they quickly went to their tertiary site and then went to ground. Literally. The team spent the next 48 hours in a very shallow eighteen-inch subsurface hide, on their backs, shoulder to shoulder, with a camouflage canvas sheet spray painted the same color as the sand, covering all six of them. They lay there and saw the Iraqi soldiers walk right past them, no more than ten feet away. If the long-range surveillance team had shot at them, it would have turned into a gunfight and our team would have lost because they were significantly outnumbered and the good guys, the cavalry, were 800km away in Kuwait.

"Thankfully, we went on to recover all three teams without any casualties. At one point during their surveillance mission, one long-range surveillance team came up on the Victory Command Network with their SALUTE (Size Activity Location Unit Time and Equipment) report. The net control, the non-commissioned officer in charge of the network, ensured communications were operational for the corps commander and they immediately said, 'Get off this net, this is the corps commander's net your stepping in.' The corps commander overheard and said. 'Hey! That's my long-range surveillance team.'

"They sent this SALUTE report which contained information about a number of technical vehicles with big heavy gauge machine guns mounted in the back, moving south in the vicinity of Objective Rams. By this time, the invasion was ongoing and as soon as that report came in, the 3rd Infantry Division commander got involved and called in Apaches, destroying all those technical vehicles. That's exactly what a long-range surveillance team is supposed to do. They are inserted, they hide, watch and report back to the commander."

Recognizing the risk posed by the Bedouin dogs, at a later date Walters made a formal recommendation to reduce the probability of similar episodes reoccurring: "The recommendation was more a general note that we needed the capability to silence dogs that were barking when a long-range surveillance team was trying to hide and perform their task. The recommendation was that we used silenced weapons.

"For conventional units, having silenced weapons was not common at all. For special operations units it happened routinely, because they would often need to get in quietly and if something came up that was going to make some noise, they needed to be able to engage that threat in a stealthy manner without notifying everyone in the area that they were present.

"A silenced weapon still performs as it's designed, except it's not as loud when you shoot. You can still hear the charging mechanism, if it's an M-4 or M-16 for example, that's gas operated. When you squeeze the trigger, the round goes out, the bolt is slammed to the rear, and it goes back in to put the next round in the chamber. You can still hear that mechanical action take place, but what you don't hear is that loud crack when a round goes out with a weapon that's not silenced, which can ultimately give away your position."

Major Edwards added: "The common term in the military is suppressor as opposed to silencer, which is a civilian term or one that you are most likely to see in a film. It suppresses the muzzle flash and the noise, which are otherwise clear giveaways of where you are at when shooting. That gives you an added level of security. From the dog perspective, and I learned this later, all the Bedouin camps that are free flowing around Iraq, the majority used dogs as their security. They'd keep maybe ten or twenty dogs in their camp, which would notify those in the camp of coyotes and other predators on their livestock, which was something of monetary value to the camp and in essence could take away their livelihood. Goats, camels, chickens etc."

Walters continued: "The feral dogs were more a case of health and safety once we got to Balad because these dogs were running rampant all over the Iraqi Air Force base. They were rabid and would often bite people. There was a military veterinarian there, who was in charge of eliminating these feral dogs, but he didn't have a means to do it, so he asked us if we would help.

"What we did was, we had a group of long-range surveillance guys with a couple of Humvees and they would pull alongside these dogs and then start chasing them in their vehicle. There would be a non-commissioned officer in charge of each vehicle and that officer would direct one of the soldiers to shoot the dog. But you had to be careful about what you did because you were on a friendly base. You had to make sure you were shooting down at the dogs, so you'd hit the animal and the round would go into the ground. We would then put the dead dog in the back of the vehicle which the veterinarians drove around in and they would then take the carcasses and burn them."

Major Edwards recalled: "When I arrived in June of 2003, we were still doing this. You'd see dogs with three legs, one eye, half a tail and all kinds of stuff going on. You had to take care of it from a health and hygiene perspective. There was no other way around it, because if you've been bitten, there's no effective cure for rabies.

"In 2010, when I was battalion commander, I was out doing a Bedouin engagement and was sitting in this guy's tent on the ground drinking some tea. He had multiple camps around our forward operating base, so I wanted to meet with him to forge an amicable relationship between the Army and his people. I had a military police soldier with me who was carrying a shotgun and we had loaded the shotgun with beanbag ammunition, which is a non-lethal round. One of his dogs was getting too close and she got nervous and shot it with the beanbag. The round didn't kill the dog, but the guy got really mad at me, because that was his area. As Bob said, these are not pets. These are wild animals. Better safe than sorry."

The issue of feral dogs would rear its canine head again further down the line in 2003, but by that stage it was the least of their worries. For now, the war against terror and dictatorship in Iraq was the priority.

5

Summer of 2003

"The two sons of Saddam Hussein, Uday and Qusay, have been killed by U.S. troops in Iraq. The bodies of the two men were identified after two hundred American soldiers, backed by helicopters, stormed a house in the northern city of Mosul following a tip-off from an Iraqi informant."

—BBC News

On July 22, 2003, Uday and Qusay Hussein were killed during a raid. They were recognized by many as being more barbaric and stone hearted than their infamous father Saddam and their deaths led to city-wide celebrations across the streets of Baghdad. LTC Walters recalled the intelligence which ultimately signposted the U.S. Army to the Husseins' location: "We had a human intelligence team up at the airbase in Mosul by the entry control point and we were just a supporting element of the unit. While we were there, we had a place where walk-ins could come. People with information they wanted to share regarding the coalition.

"At the time, we had a young soldier at the airbase who was about eighteen-years-old and one day an Iraqi walk-in arrived. This guy said, 'I've got these two people that have taken over my house and I'm not happy about it and I'm sure they're related to Saddam Hussein. I want you guys to help me get rid of them because they are mistreating my family. I'm very nervous because I know they'll kill me if they know I'm speaking to you guys.

"The specialist did an amazing job after the initial contact. He took this information to his boss, who was a sergeant and gave him some guidance. We didn't know who these bad guys were but based on the report we also didn't know if the source was legitimate or not. Maybe the guy was just showing up to get some money out of the coalition. The guidance to the young specialist was to meet this guy again and get additional information, like where exactly his house was at and who exactly these two characters were who were staying at his house and tormenting him and his family.

"The specialist set up the revisit, the Iraqi guy came back, and he got all the additional information from him. This was put into a report and given to the 101st along with the Special Operational Joint Task Force 7, who then did the raid on the house and killed Saddam Hussein's sons. That was all based on a walk-in to a young specialist in a very hostile and austere environment, just doing his job and doing it, very, very well. This kid recognized that this guy was legitimate. If he hadn't recognized that, there was no telling how long it would have been before we would have got to Saddam Hussein's sons. The 101st Airborne Division commander eventually pinned the impact Bronze Star award on our specialist."

Edwards added: "What's important to mention here is that this was a 165th soldier from our battalion in one of the biggest takedowns of the conflict at the time and as a battalion, we were very proud of him."

The 165th was geographically dispersed over Iraq, matching their personnel to the most critical needs, which included having soldiers based at the fabled Green Zone. The area was approximately 10km squared, based in the Karkh area of Central Baghdad and after the U.S. invasion, was a very difficult place to access, behind its high fortified blast walls and barbed wire fences. As far as Iraq goes, it was one of the safer places to be inside. Edwards recalled his first visit in August 2003: "Myself, the operations officer and Bob would go to places where we had soldiers. This is called battlefield circulation. The 165th's headquarters were in Balad, but the battalion was spread out all over the area of operations in Iraq, which meant we were embedded with the 101st, the 3rd Armored Cavalry Regiment out in Anbar, etc, supporting other units with whichever skillset. We would check if our soldiers were living okay, had everything they needed and were executing their respective operations.

"At this point we were months into the deployment and our living conditions at Balad weren't bad but were certainly not the best. I had a washtub in the little place that I slept at, and I'd take my clothes on a washboard and wash them in that tub. That was the environment. We did the best we could with what we had. The Green Zone was different.

"First time I landed there, I was sitting in this Black Hawk and I kind of fell asleep. I was on some headsets with the pilot, and I woke up and said while looking out of the window, 'What is that?' We were just sitting on the helicopter landing zone and the rotors were turning as they were picking someone up. Outside, there were young professionals carrying briefcases wearing suits and nice business dress, walking around demonstrating normal life activity. It was very surreal. I'd come from a highly tactical austere environment in Balad, to what felt like the central business district of Baghdad."

LTC Walters added: "The best way I can describe it is, when you leave Baghdad and the Green Zone in particular, you're out in the rural countryside and it's austere for everybody, including the Iraqi citizens living in the area. A lot of them lived in mud huts and that was normal. They'd take mud, build a wall around their huts and then they'd use whatever construction materials available and make these things by hand. When we had gotten there, the Iraqi military had taken all the stuff that they wanted before they abandoned the base, so when we arrived, we had to start from the bottom up.

"But when you got into the Green Zone, this area was protected by both the U.S. and host nation security forces. This is where the Iraqi elite lived. Not only did they conduct their business, but they looked the part. If you'd just spent the last three months living out in the dirt and you're in the helicopter and it lands in the Green Zone, it can be a surprise for you, to say the least."

Reflecting on the rougher side of the coin, Edwards recalled an episode shortly after visiting the Green zone that same summer: "Around early September, Bob asked me to go down to Ramadi for a couple of weeks, where we had long-range surveillance teams who were working with the 3rd Armored Cavalry Regiment (ACR), which was a regiment that was a land owner of that portion of Iraq at the time. They were a big unit who were self-sustained with all necessary combat capabilities and Bob wanted me to let him know how things were going with their mission.

"One evening I accompanied one of the long-range surveillance patrols down to the banks of the river as they prepared for a night boat insertion for a mission that evening. As the team prepared on the riverbank for the small boat to show up, I asked if we had coordinated and de-conflicted with the ACR's attack aviation. The river was patrolled nightly by Apaches. There was a moment of silence, so I headed back to the tactical operation center to make sure the mission was logged with the Apache unit. Fortunately, all was good, but I did have a moment of panic worrying they would be mistaken for the enemy. I made it back to the pick-up location and jumped on the boat to observe the insertion. After the team was out, the boat driver took me back up to the link-up point. The team made it back without incident and we started another day of planning for patrols.

"Sleeping arrangement were interesting on this mission. I went down there with a group of long-range surveillance soldiers and non-commissioned officers and the team areas were packed with LRS soldiers, so I ended up staying in the headquarters area of the 3rd ACR, near their tactical operation center, which was a series of buildings that overlooked some palaces of Saddam Hussein's sons. The first couple of nights, the guys from cavalry were like, 'If you can take a cot out there, that would be good.' I said, 'Okay. No problem.' I got my cot out of the Humvee and set it up next to the building. What they didn't tell me was that it was next to the air refueling point for all the Apaches that were flying in and going out for night missions.

"I didn't get a great sleep and when I woke up the next morning, I had about two inches of dust all over my sleeping bag and had to dig myself out of it. What happened was, these helicopters had been on a patrol mission of the river all night long and the rotor wash had been blowing all over me. I slept next to the refueling point for a few more days and then made the wise decision to move my cot to a quieter spot. Nothing like rotor wash to remind you of the power of an Apache.

"Another story relating to noise in this mission involved a standing open-top freezer in the tactical operations center, which had a sign on it that said, 'Don't let the lid drop.' Well, one day we were in there and one of the cavalry soldiers opened the freezer to get a bottle of water and then let the lid drop. It sounded exactly like a mortar round and many of the people in that area were heading under tables for cover. It was funny but true for the environment we were working and living in."

The noise from the Apache may have made sleeping an arduous task, but the wake-up call they were about to receive far superseded any rotor wash.

6

Call to Action

"The battalion had a specially trained infantry, recon-
naissance unit. There was great confidence in the
strong leadership and capability of the 165th. Of all of
our units, from a functionality and leadership perspec-
tive, they were really the only choice for this mission."
—Major Mickie Williams

On August 7, 2003, the Jordanian embassy was bombed in Baghdad, followed by the UN headquarters twelve days later. Then on October 14, the Turkish embassy took a hit, followed soon after by the
bombing of the Rasheed hotel, a well known spot for U.S. journalists
to stay, nestled nicely into Baghdad's Green Zone. Fifteen people were
injured, and one U.S. soldier perished.

As Baghdad fell, outbreaks of regional violence occurred throughout Iraq; however, on the whole, the U.S. Army was unaffected. LTC
Walters explained. "Early on during the invasion, the Iraqi populace was
settling grudges. Iraqi on Iraqi violence. We would move through areas
where some people would cheer us and then we'd go through to the next
village, and they would look at us with disdain. It depended on what
kind of thoughts they had about the coalition. By and large, after the
Iraqi Army fell, we were not the targets. That certainly changed later
though.

"At that point, the insurgency was forming, and this was like the
beginning of Al Qaeda Iraq (AQI), right there. Those were some of the
activities the terrorist were conducting. Here's how it impacted us. The
long-range surveillance guys would be looking for terrorist activities,
establishing things that terrorists would use to disrupt coalition forces.
At the same time, our tactical human teams would be collecting human
intelligence on the network and providing that to help us build a puzzle of what that network looked like, then that information was pushed

up to higher headquarters and units were tasked to do something about those networks. That information was then pushed to the interrogators at corps and they would use it to fill in the missing pieces of the puzzle. If we didn't understand the network, we were going to be ineffective in countering the insurgency."

Major Edwards added: "The summer of '03 from say June to August was pretty quiet. There was a bubble, a time period when we were in Balad and the high intensity conflict was over and we were thinking, 'When are we going home? We've done our mission.'

"We were doing a lot of internal work, staying vigilant, doing patrolling missions, keeping the area of operation under our control and coordination with the brigade combat team that was on Balad at the time. Then when IEDs became prevalent in the summer of '03, that was a game changer. Up to then, we were driving all over the place in June and July, going to Ramadi, Baghdad, you name it and we had to have our wits about us and do our techniques properly, but in those days, we were driving around in Humvees with no doors. We then went into a whole mission of countering the IED and all kinds of technology solutions started to pop up and creative ideas from soldiers on how to maneuver the battle space in that type of environment."

IEDs came with deadly consequences and so did the mission the 165th were about to be deployed on. Edwards recalled what he aptly named Black Wednesday: "It was late October 2003, and we were in the tactical operations center in Balad. Bob, myself, the operations officer, the sergeant major, assistant operations officer, operations sergeant major, the intel officer. It was an Iraqi, cinder block type of building where we were set up. On the desk we had our laptops, which allowed us to communicate with other military personnel, although we weren't connected to the internet and didn't have access to emails, Skype or any of that stuff, because the infrastructure was destroyed. We were working off military communications backbones. We were talking to each other, but not the outside world.

"On this particular Wednesday, we had this Army tactical phone on a desk between myself, Bob and the sergeant major. The phone rings, I pick it up. It was Major Mickie Williams from Baghdad. He had a new mission for us. Normally, you'd get mission directions, a purpose, some kind of structure, but on this occasion, we had none of that."

Taking a small step back, Major Mickie Williams shared his story, which led to "that" call: "The brigade commander, myself, the sergeant major were all part of the command team for the brigade. We were at Camp Victory at the headquarters when the 800th MP brigade commander walked in. We had been kind of told that there was consideration for turning over Abu Ghraib as a forward operating base to us. Some of us resisted that. We were already doing intel ops across Iraq at the time and just did not feel the 800th Military Police Brigade were suited for running a forward operating base, an interrogation operation, plus all the other types of intel work we were doing across Iraq. Nevertheless, there were some significant concerns on leadership and security at Abu Ghraib. There had been a series of intel reporting that the prisoners there were planning a breakout. The 800th commander informed our commander and myself that she and the Combined Joint Task Force 7 commander had justified it to give the forward operating base over to the 205th.

"Our brigade commander and I immediately started asking how we were going to do this. The bottom line came down to needing to have some form of headquarters there but did not think that the brigade headquarters should be at that location. That then led to conversations about our other battalions and who had the largest force that could tighten up the security.

"Back to October 2003. Our brigade commander and I decided that we would split the brigade staff with regards to Abu Ghraib, to take over the forward operating base from a colonel level, with Bob and his battalion there to sure up the security and carry out what was needed day in, day out. Myself and the executive officer were left with the rest of the brigade back at Balad. That then led to a call to Bill."

EDWARDS: Hey Mickie. What's happening?
WILLIAMS: Hi Bill. We need the 165th to go to Abu Ghraib.
EDWARDS: I looked at Bob and said, "They've just told us to move the battalion to Abu Ghraib."
WALTERS: What? When? Get more information.
EDWARDS: Mickie. What's the mission? What's the task?
WILLIAMS: Just fix it!

Walters added further context to the responsibilities of Williams at the time: "He was the 205th brigade operations officer, was our higher headquarters operations officer and was running the 205th tactical operations center. He had multiple battalions and the 165th was just one of them. He wasn't just running the brigade, he was running multiple operations in a combat zone. This included an aerial exploitation battalion, which was flown on a daily basis and that included the 519th, a military intelligence battalion, and then he had reserve and national guard augmentation. At one point there were about five battalions under the 205th that Mickie was running on a daily basis. He had a tremendous responsibility and the 165th was just a part of that.

"When Mickie gave orders to more senior officers, that was routine. It wasn't this major is going to tell me what to do, it was more like, this major has been directed by the brigade commander to run the brigade while the brigade commander is doing other duties. When Mickie called out, 'Hey guys, we got something for you,' he was always professional and polite. He had a difficult job and we understood that and he performed very well. We responded as we did, as if the brigade commander was calling."

Edwards continued: "That call ingrained into my mind. It's one I never forgot. We put a plan together to go out and do an assessment of the security. We knew there were some concerns, but again, we were part of an intel apparatus that was already operating there, in terms of interrogation operation. At that point, the brigade commander was spending a fair amount of time at Abu Ghraib because the Combined Joint Task Force 7 commander really wanted an increased presence. Again, we knew something, but we didn't know the total situation.

"You have to bear in mind we had to move over four hundred people, all the equipment and over one hundred vehicles. The logistics behind that, a timeline, everything had to happen sequentially to get an

Battalion commander's weekly update to the troops prior to the Change of Mission to Abu Ghraib (William Edwards' collection).

46

organization moved from an operating base to a place that was far from that. When we eventually got down there, we had to build the entire infrastructure, just so we could operate. We came up with a plan and bounced it off Bob and he told us to get moving."

While the 165th prepared to carry out reconnaissance at Abu Ghraib, the families back at base in Germany were confronting their own battles connected to their loved one's mission.

Initial Infrastructure Improvement—a massive effort to create driveable roads and lessen the mud (William Edwards' collection).

7

Embrace the Suck

"If you look at the movies and read books, they always talk about the guys that are downrange. However, a real key aspect to the story that frequently goes unnoticed are the spouses and children back home that are constantly being asked for interviews and are living and reacting to those media stories."
—Major General Robert P. Walters, Jr.

Prisons such as Guantanamo Bay and Abu Ghraib were continuously in the headlines in the early 2000s. For the loved ones, they were never far from watching, hearing or reading a headline which could ignite fear and anxiety.

On August 25, 2004, the *New York Times* reported:

Of the 17 detention facilities in Iraq, the largest, Abu Ghraib, housed up to 7,000 detainees in October 2003, with a guard force of only about 90 personnel from the 800th Military Police Brigade. Abu Ghraib was seriously overcrowded, under-resourced, and under continual attack. Five U.S. soldiers died as a result of mortar attacks on Abu Ghraib. In July 2003, Abu Ghraib was mortared 25 times.

Unfortunately, those violently volatile statistics continued to rise in the coming months as LTC Walters and Major Edwards embarked on their mission.

Walters' wife, Nancy, recalled, "Wondering if I would get to kiss him again when we said goodbye for deployment was the one single biggest challenge of being the spouse of a military serviceman. However, Abu Ghraib was the one assignment that was a gut puncher. The rest of them were the regular highs and lows of a military family, but that deployment was the one that blindsided us.

"Not having regular contact made it worse. Bob was always good at communicating to us. He was a very good letter writer and would always have a notebook in his pocket. What is interesting, is due to the longevity of my husband's career, our ways to communicate evolved from radio, letters, phone and emails, but when he got to Abu Ghraib, it didn't matter which technology was available, because it came down to when Bob would have a chance to get in touch. When you're watching or reading the news, you start to wonder when that next opportunity might be, if at all."

Walters added: "The thing about Abu Ghraib was that we didn't know the length of the deployment from the outset. Our family members all wanted to know when we were coming back, but we simply had no knowledge to depart with. That was a constant state we operated in. Normally, we'd have replacement personnel coming in like Bill then we'd send people back to Germany and they'd get assigned to other places.

"But with Abu Ghraib, if you weren't due to rotate out of Germany, you stayed in Iraq with the battalion and you didn't know when you were going back. At this point, we'd hope we were going to go home by Thanksgiving, then that became Christmas. There was no incoming unit coming up behind us, so Christmas would come and go and we wouldn't know when we were going home."

Assistant Operations Officer Mike Flentie recalled: "We didn't have communications like you do now. You talked to your spouse very rarely and I did not lay eyes on my wife for a year after landing in Iraq. Everybody else was in the same situation. I can't imagine what was going through their minds because all they saw was the wounded coming back. They were very tight knit and took care of each other, but they had it rough."

Outside of her father's communication, Daytona pulled no punches in expressing her view about what the media were reporting: "I generally stopped watching the news whenever he was deployed. I didn't think I could trust any news station on what was happening. I had enough feelings to navigate, I didn't need news commentary reminding me there were dangerous situations going on in the world. I never feared the news or the 'knock on the door,' it was always the phone calls that made me anxious. I was worried I was going to pick up the phone and there would be bad news. Every time dad left for deployment, we would pray that we didn't get that phone call. My personal thoughts were a messy mix of desperately wanting him home, fear of him getting killed, anger at him leaving, gratitude for his service, and wanting the tightness in my chest to go away."

Sister, Martina concurred: "I stopped watching the news. I still don't very much to this day. I remember a reporter approaching us one day asking questions I did not have the answers to, nor did I feel it was any of their business. Even as a child, I was unimpressed with the dramatic flair presented in those situations. What my dad was doing out there was Army stuff, keeping the fight off American soil. That was all I needed to know. I don't remember having a desire to know specifics."

Major Edwards' daughter, Madeline, shared a similar mindset but also discussed some coping mechanisms: "During his first deployment I was worried about his welfare, but only with the capacity of a nine or ten-year-old. I knew something could happen, but I couldn't fully understand it. It was still stressful but in a more abstract way. During his second deployment, I did not watch the news, because there was just too much negativity surrounding them and I didn't want to hear about the war. I would rather live in my little bubble, in which I worked very hard to be happy and fulfilled. That may be a bit selfish, but it is how I dealt with it. Aside from being stressful if someone was injured or died, it also hurt me when people on TV had negative opinions about the war. The Iraq war was very polarizing, and I didn't want to hear people's opinions about it. It hit too close to home."

From a parent's perspective trying to shield their children from media came with its challenges. Nancy explained: "In addition to taking into account age appropriateness, the biggest challenge with the evolution of 24-hour news and the internet was making sure they were not broadsided or caught off guard, especially because first reports are never the factual ones. As they got older, they knew what was at stake. Our family motto was 'Embrace the Suck.' We actually have T-shirts! Sometimes we knew we would have to go through episodes that sucked, so we just embraced it to get to the other side. At that point, the suck was the Operation Iraqi Freedom 1 deployment, which was a real beast.

"Germany did not support the United States involvement in Iraq and didn't have organizations in the country to support us. Most of the families couldn't afford to leave Germany and come back to the U.S. and others didn't even have family back in the U.S. because they had their families with them. They had to stay and deal with it. What we would do was organize different trips in Europe to get into the culture, but that abruptly stopped when the war broke out. Instead, each week all we did was put out warnings. 'Don't stop in this area. Don't buy your groceries from this area, because the protesting is going to be significant there this week.' That's how quickly things changed and yes, it did suck."

Nancy candidly continued: "And to address the question of physical illnesses, I am the poster child. I currently have two machines implanted in my body, one for a congenital heart condition but the other because I have had more surgeries in my abdomen than I can count. The level of stress that comes with deployments and especially as the command spouse in an active deployment is hard. *But,* I would do it again and support it again because it is a unique calling that serves a much greater purpose.

"Folks that have never been associated with the military or cannot fathom how a soldier or their family does it, sometimes believe that we must get used to it. Nothing is farther from the truth. Deployments are open wounds that never get to heal before another one begins. It is an unhealed scab that keeps getting ripped off. Every deployment had its effects, especially when loss was involved.

"It never got easier, there was absolutely nothing we could do about it, but there is a phenomenon that seasoned spouses were aware of. Couples would argue over anything and everything, because it was easier to say goodbye to someone who you were mad at."

As the number of deployments increased over the years, thankfully, so did the level and understanding of support from the U.S. Army, although the scope for improvement is still ongoing. Nancy explained: "The Army's assistance became greater and greater with lessons learned from each deployment. They had multiple agencies in place, toll free numbers to call for mental health support, financial assistance and more. Was it perfect? No. But it was not from lack of effort by the Army. The support and organizations put in place by the military were good, however the ever changing and growing needs of military families going through repeat deployments has been an ongoing challenge. Childcare for military spouses is a great need. There are never enough qualified childcare givers, which is an issue to this day. And military medical facilities were and continue to be challenged in having enough doctors and specialists to meet the demand especially at remote installations."

Martina added: "My mom is a remarkable human being. We called ourselves the Core 4 and she was the backbone of that. She managed my sister and I through each move every two years as we said goodbye to friends and familiar spaces, and set up our new houses in record time making it look like we had lived there for years. She did an incredible job."

Keeping mentally focused and adopting the "Charlie Mike," mind-set is all well and good, but in reality, how easy was it to maintain a sane focus? Nancy explained: "During the deployments there were up and down days. I think I was too busy treading water to have time to be depressed. But down times, really down times they were definitely salt and peppered throughout.

"I think the fishbowl life of a commander's spouse and family prob-ably helped to not allow me to get stuck in it. A commander spouse really does not have the luxury of getting to vent the way you really would like to. A wise senior spouse once told me, in command, the first thing I needed to be very discerning of, was someone that was trust-worthy and even then, to be guarded. I was always blessed to have a friend that I could trust during each deployment that was outside of our unit. For Operation Iraqi Freedom 1, I had a chaplain's wife that was extremely proactive in making sure I was alright. I believe her friendship was what kept me on track."

When Major Edwards received notice of his imminent deploy-ment to Iraq, the relocation happened expeditiously, but not without its issues. Dana recalled: "During this time there was no literature or counselling for the deployment. The unit was already downrange when Bill received his orders. We were originally supposed to move to Hei-delberg and consequently I spent a lot of time researching housing, activities and schools before our move. Our furniture and all of our belongings were already packed up and on their way. We were in a hotel awaiting our flight to Heidelberg when Bill received an email that said he was assigned to be the executive officer for the 165th Battalion in Iraq. There was very little time to prepare or explain to the girls what was going on."

Coining the phrase, 'Hitting the ground running,' Dana explained her extensive preparations for driving in Germany. "I knew that when we landed, Bill was going to leap for an undetermined amount of time and I needed to be mobile and drive the girls to school or their activities. So, we studied for the German driving test on the plane ride over."

Edwards added: "Germany required those serving in the U.S. mil-itary to pass what was called a U.S. Army European driving test. We landed about 6am in Frankfurt and they had transportation arranged

Edwards family photo around the time of Operation Iraqi Freedom. From left: Madeline, Elise, Dana and Bill (William Edwards' collection).

where they took me directly to the U.S. base that did the testing. The idea was for me to take my driver's test the day we landed, pass and be able to drive in the country immediately."

Walters commented: "That test was no joke. Everybody had to take it to drive in Germany. The symbology part of it had about sixty questions and you had to nail it or you didn't pass. It was a rite of passage to being assigned to Germany."

Edwards continued: "At the time, I had a friend of mine who was waiting for me at the driver's testing site, to loan me one of his cars if I passed, so the pressure was on. Even inside the family unit they were planning like it was a military operation! That car would come in very handy as my personal vehicle didn't arrive for several months.

"In order to pass you had to know all the road signs and the rules of the road, which are very different to the U.S. I turned my exam in at a place called Babenhausen to an older German guy and he graded it right there in front of me. It was about a hundred questions, and I said, 'Am I good?' and he said with a deadpan face in true German fashion, 'No, but you passed.' Dana took the test a day or two later and also passed, then I left for Iraq, leaving everything else on her shoulders.

"I have to say, Dana was great. She jumped right in and learned as much as she could very quickly and got involved. There's a lot of unwritten rules that a U.S. military officer lives by. When you're in the Army, they get two for one, because they employ the spouses so much, that it's as if they should be paid for what they do, specifically with the family assistance groups and family readiness group of the unit and all the volunteering they are required to do.

"When I was stationed at Fort Riley, Kansas, I was in a heavy Armor battalion and I was getting my officer evaluation report by the colonel and he called me into his office and he said, 'Your wife is a fantastic representative of our unit and you're going to get a good officer evaluation report.' Although he said this half-jokingly, he was, to an extent, basing my rating on Dana's performance in that unit, because his wife liked my wife. It was one of those times I walked out of there, like an epiphany and thought, 'Wow.' As I got more senior in the Army, the requirements for her grew immensely.

"When I was a battalion commander a number of years later, I had an eight-hundred-man battalion in Iraq and we were gone fourteen months. Dana was running all the back-end stuff at home. Eight hundred soldiers and more or less five hundred of them had family in Colorado, where we were based out of and she had to organize all these events throughout the year like, Thanksgiving, Christmas, Easter etc. Not to mention they were required to do a once a week meeting with spouses. If your wife just didn't participate and said, 'I've got other things to do,' in the early days that would have been a discriminator for you as an officer. It's an interesting culture to say the least."

Dana added: "I have no military in my family. It was a really foreign world to me. There's a lot of rules and protocol. Being a cohabitant was frowned upon and many of the wives of the military told me that if I wanted to stay with Bill, I'd need to get married to him.

"When I did get married, I was given a handbook of etiquette for military spouses. What to wear for a change of command, how to address a general and identifying different ranks. After I had Madeline and she was maybe three months old, someone else in the unit needed a baby shower and they said, 'It's your turn. You're up.' It didn't matter that I had a three-month-old baby, you just got on and did it. You took turns. There was a lot of voluntary obligation, important things though and things I enjoyed doing, but I'd never been a part of something like that before. It was different when you grew up in your family and what you chose to give your personal time to or charity, because these were obligations."

Nancy explained: "When Bob was first deployed for Desert Storm in 1990, the military didn't provide any literature or counselling in preparation for spouses leaving. Out of Desert Storm came family support groups. Overtime it was changed to family readiness groups. But no one was ready for Operation Iraqi Freedom 1 in 2003.

"At the pre-command course that Bob and I attended before he took command in Germany, the training for the family readiness groups and battalion command spouses was more on the legal guidelines for bake sales and organizing team building events for families. Back then, the guidance was very minimal for the spouses."

Back to adapting in Europe for Operation Iraqi Freedom 1, Dana recalled: "It was certainly an adjustment driving in Germany. They had very strict rules driving on the autobahn. If you drive slower, you stick to the right and if you want to pass another car, it's only on the left. Also, there's no speed limit on the autobahn. The language wasn't too much of a barrier for me as I speak German, the most challenging part of driving was not having maps or sat nav. If my daughter had a soccer game in a field somewhere, it was a case of being lost all the time."

Madeline added: "I often felt like I was on an Army mission because I was ten years old, in the front seat with no map reading skills, unable to speak German using a giant paper map as the key navigator to get my mom, sister and myself to my soccer games on time."

Dana continued: "If we had a holiday or a long weekend we'd often travel with the other families, in order for my girls not to feel so isolated because their dad wasn't home. I drove to France, Poland, Italy and in Germany, and you can kind of make sense of things like exits, but I did get lost a lot.

"The other issue was housing. When we arrived in Darmstadt, there wasn't any housing available onsite, so we were given a third-floor apartment in Langen, approximately thirty minutes or longer with autobahn traffic, from Darmstadt. Raising two young girls in a small apartment without air conditioning in one of the hottest summers in European history was not easy. Also, this particular move and deployment was complicated by the fact our furniture and belongings had been shipped and designated for Heidelberg, which isn't helpful when you are living 75km away in Langen. Then, half of our shipment could not be located and there were no partial deliveries, so we just lived for months out of our suitcases and what we had shipped in hold baggage. The girls and I still laugh about how much fun we had camped in the empty apartment. I thought at the time we probably had too much stuff anyway and you need very little to be happy.

"As the old expression goes, life goes on and you had to suck it up. The commissary, mailroom, and small post exchange were located in Darmstadt so my daily tasks of getting mail and groceries involved a lot of commuting, sometimes to find out the mail had not arrived. Then I'd do it all again the next day. It was a lot of in and out of the car seat for Elise who was three at the time. However, I have fond memories of driving and singing to the Lilo and Stitch soundtrack, with Elise belting out Elvis's 'Burning Love.'

"Holding down the fort was a lot of pressure, and it was heightened by the fact we were in a foreign country. Being the sole person responsible for the safety and wellbeing of your children is a tremendous responsibility. The key to maintaining normalcy for me was having a stable routine. Madeline attended art classes, played soccer and rode equestrian, and Elise took gymnastics.

Dana (center), Madeline (right) and Elise (left), bike ride in Langen, 2003 (William Edwards' collection).

"Elise tried German preschool, but it was too much change at once and her separation anxiety was too great to be away from me. I discussed it with her pediatrician and he said it was like a grieving process for her. She still thought her dad was lost in the airport and although I reassured her that her dad was at work, she just could not comprehend why we did not see him or talk to him anymore. Whenever she would see another soldier in uniform, I could see her get so excited because she thought it might be her dad. That was heart breaking to watch.

"To make it worse, the communication with Bill was very limited. Our internet in our apartment did not work and scheduling with the German phone company was frustrating. One of the soldiers from the unit tried to fix it but to no avail. I had to drive to Darmstadt to go to the library to check and send emails. The problem was resolved after several months, but the communication with Bill was almost non-existent.

"I really did not share many details of what Bill endured in Iraq with Madeline and Elise, but that was also due to the fact that I did not actually know a lot of details due to the lack of communication. We spoke very little. Maybe once or twice. I didn't know what was going on. One of the calls, he was patched through the rear detachment and there was an incident which involved casualties. They told me he was fine and to be confident that the situation was under control, and everyone was getting the care they needed and they were dealing with the fatality. They wanted me to know, because they didn't want my mind to wander out of control, because news and rumors spread very fast.

"That phone call was very brief, and my reaction was relief to hear his voice after so many months, but I mainly felt fear for him. I needed more information knowing he was okay and that simply wasn't available. I am not really sure how I coped with it other than putting it out of my mind and going about what needed to be done with daily tasks with the house, laundry, cooking, homework with Madeline, reading to Elise and playing board games together and getting them to their activities.

Elise recalled: "My mom always kept us distracted. She was the only one in the know and she never projected that stress on us. I had these Pooh Bear puppets and one time my mom and I left one of the puppets in Poland and we went back to Poland to get it. She never wanted us to worry and was always positive for us."

Dana continued: "We were fortunate to have a few wonderful neighbors that we would have dinner with and watch a weekly television program and that was a great distraction. However, I had a neighbor who was trying to sympathize with Bill being gone and she told me, even though her husband was home he was 'deployed in place.' I think she was trying to say, although he was back home, but because he had been working so much, he might as well be deployed. For me, there's a big difference working from home and being out in the battlefield, so I didn't have as much sympathy. I suppose people are not exactly sure what to say to comfort others during difficult times. There's no correct manuscript in those situations."

As the pressure and anxiety piled on for the families back in Germany, the 165th set off for Abu Ghraib.

8

Reconnaissance

"Time spent on reconnaissance is time seldom wasted."
—John Marsden

Major Edwards' knowledge of Abu Ghraib prior to going out to Iraq was very limited. He admitted, "I didn't even know where it was on the map." LTC Walters however had in depth peripheral knowledge: "I was aware that the Combined Joint Task Force 7, which was the senior military command in Iraq at the time, was using Abu Ghraib as a detention facility for detainees that were picked up on the battlefield.

"What would happen is a unit would go out on patrol and they would find an Iraqi, or several Iraqis that were breaking policies. Out after curfew, carrying weapons, whatever the infraction was, these guys were detained and then they would be transported to Abu Ghraib, where they would be processed.

"One of our sister units, the 519th, Military Intelligence Battalion out of Fort Bragg, North Carolina, had their alpha company at Abu Ghraib, conducting interrogations of the detainees. The purpose of the interrogations was to gather battlefield information that would assist the Combined Joint Task Force 7 in accomplishing its tactical military mission. Where are IEDs being built? Who is leading the insurgency? What is the purpose of the insurgency? What members of the former Iraqi Army are now a part of the insurgency? Those types of questions.

"I saw a fragmentary order from Combined Joint Task Force 7 which went out to all of the military forces deployed there. One of the commands on that order was for the commander of the 205th Military Intelligence Brigade, who at that time was my immediate boss, to assume command of the forward operating base in Abu Ghraib. That order came out and then we got that call."

Shortly after the call, the wheels were set in motion to relocate the

165th. Walters continued. "From the time of the phone call from Mickie, we had a convoy out the next day. I called the brigade commander and he said, 'Hey Bob, I need you guys down here tomorrow to do an initial reconnaissance,' and that's what we did."

Major Edwards added: "I was with Bob and the team that arrived 24 hrs later. We did the call late in the evening and the next morning we were rolling in a combat patrol that was put together with the leadership of the battalion and from our long-range surveillance company.

"Major Mickie Williams met us at Abu Ghraib on the ground and it was the same nebulous mission direction. 'Just fix this place! Get it up to standard. Get things under control.'"

Amidst the start of a serious mission, Major Edwards recalled a light hearted moment: "Bob had a great head of hair back then and still does now. The journey from Balad to Abu Ghraib took us a couple of hours driving down this crazy highway and there we were wearing our helmets and protective equipment. We were just starting to see the advent of the IED, which was a new concept in those days, and we were doing things like driving in the middle of the road to give us space from the side of the road and checking the side of the road for garbage piles or any other indicators that might indicate a bomb was there. In reality that would have never helped us against such a devastating explosive device, but it made us feel good, so we did it.

"So, there we were, driving as fast as we could to get down there, all tensed up, looking for things. We get down to Abu Ghraib, get out of the vehicle, then Bob takes off his helmet and his hair is perfect! He was cool and calm, which was exactly what you need in a battalion commander.

"Back to Abu Ghraib. My first thought as we arrived at the entry control point was, 'Something isn't right.' There was a single Humvee sitting there with two U.S. soldiers in it and five Iraqi women, wearing full burkas, hovering around the vehicle. You don't have an entry control point set up with just one Humvee, no material around it to protect you, no gun positions and no way to screen people to get in. As the U.S. Army, at our entry control points, everything was done in a very rigid, controlled, military manner, because it's such a critical place. It's the opening into your perimeter. You have to protect that. This was the complete opposite. Anyone could have just driven through with a vehicle-borne IED and killed a bunch of people."

Walters added: "Abu Ghraib was a horrible, horrible place and what Bill aptly mentioned was indicative of the current poor discipline and weak security posture. We identified several things that needed to be upgraded immediately on the perimeter security. As we drove past the military control point into an area where we were going to park our vehicles, I noticed a large area inside the walled compound where literally thousands of Iraqi detainees were walking around aimlessly. There were hundreds of tents set up and they had been doing laundry, which was draped across the tent ropes on tops of the tents. Also, to the north, the wall was in disrepair, meaning I could see where the wall was previously constructed, and it had crumbled apart. You could see traffic outside the compound through this significant gaping rocket hole where a gate used to be on the west side. The hole was next to a town, so people were just walking and driving in. Bear in mind this wall was supposed to serve as a perimeter boundary to keep insurgents out of the forward operating base, but it seemed like anyone could go in when they wanted. It was like a sieve.

"Lighting on the perimeter was inadequate and we also needed to put up a sniper blind, which was a screen on one portion of the wall, because there was an Iraqi civilian apartment complex next to it that was several stories higher than the prison's wall. Conceivably a sniper could be up there and take shots at U.S. soldiers inside the perimeter. We would need cement barriers to make it difficult for an attacker to get past the entry control point to launch an assault and in addition, we would need places where vehicles could be inspected, so if there was a vehicle-borne IED and it went off, it would minimize the amount of damage caused to the friendly forces. What we needed was almost the complete opposite of what was currently operational in Abu Ghraib."

Thankfully, the crumbling skeleton of the prison and its shoddy infrastructure was enough to keep the detainees from escaping. Walters explained: "The detainees were inside a fenced area inside the walled compound. They would have to get through the fence, which meant getting past towers which were manned by the military police from the 320th Battalion, which were stationed there. There was also a second area where detainees were held in what they called the 'hard stand,' which was the prison piece, internal to Abu Ghraib, where Saddam Hussein used to have prisoners who he would send there. That's where the interrogations were taking place.

"If a detainee was deemed to be high value, they would be in the hard stand facility. The interrogators had these shipping containers they were using as an interrogation area. A detainee would be escorted in by

Hard stand detainee area (William Edwards' collection).

the military police guards to the interrogation booth, then there would be an interrogator and typically an interpreter. When they were complete with interrogating the detainee, they would be taken back to wherever they were brought from."

Edwards continued: "We went into the forward operating base, Bob got all the unit leaders together around the hood of his Humvee and said, 'I have to go meet with the brigade commander and get some guidance from him. I want you guys to go out and look at logistics, sweep the compound, security, entry control point, the towers, the walls, that sort of thing. When I get done with him, we'll meet back here. I don't want to hear why this is hard or why we can't do this. I want you to tell me how we are going to do this.' Bob knew he didn't have to ask us twice. The 165th had discipline, standards and we were accountable for our actions. All those things that make a unit great. We figured out our next steps, then broke off into the complex in small teams and executed each one of those assessments, before coming back to report on our findings.

"During the reconnaissance, I took Army Captain, Romeo Qureishi down to Abu Ghraib and basically left him there. He was our logistics officer. This was not a big place, probably 1km × 1km maximum, but it was very concentrated in terms of detainee population, and it was in a terrible state. I said, 'Romeo, you have about a week and a half to get this place up to standard. I'm going back to Balad to get the battalion organized and when we come back down here, we want to fall in on functional spaces to live and to work.' Romeo did all that work himself. He was the single point of contact working with the local contractors, Muhamed, Amar and a Kurd kid, who I can't remember his name."

Captain Qureishi recalled: "The pressure to perform as the logistician at Abu Ghraib was intense. When I first got to Iraq, I was a little frustrated because I had just graduated from school and the unit had been there since February. I got to Germany, late July, early August, but I didn't leave for Iraq for about a month and a half later and that was because Major Edwards wanted to make sure that I had been to all of the requisite courses. Some of the leaders might have thought, 'Don't worry. You can learn it when you get there,' but not with Major Edwards. That was a good decision he made.

"So, I got to Iraq in October, and everybody was talking about how bad the environment was and that was true. I remember getting there on

Detainee hard stand cells (William Edwards' collection).

Spartan detainee cell (William Edwards' collection).

my first day and saw LTC Walters doing his laundry in a little washbasin. I thought, 'I guess it's pretty spartan here, for sure.' My initial impression of Abu Ghraib though, as logistician? It's like getting shot at. You don't have time to think. The order I had from Major Edwards was, 'You've got to make this liveable. It better be good, or I'm going to have your butt.' He said that with an element of humor, but the underlying factor was he wanted it to be the best it could be with whatever resources we could muster together. And that's what we did, our best.

"I was one of the first combat troops in Bosnia and that was set up fast, but in comparison to Abu Ghraib, that was a pretty small footprint. The place stunk. It was something out of Mad Max movie when we got there. There were soldiers walking around in shorts, t-shirts and flip-flops, which showed there was no discipline."

8. Reconnaissance

Edwards continued: "It's worth mentioning, when the U.S. invaded Iraq in March 2003, it was to destroy the regime that Saddam Hussein had set up, which amongst many things, supported terrorists and committed major human rights abuse against Iraqi nationals. We were at war with a dictator, but not against the whole country and its inhabitants, many of whom embraced our presence. The likes of Muhamed and Amar were good people.

"Anyway. Romeo got Muhamed to get those walls put up and get the space carved out. The position I was in, I was counting on Romeo to deliver and he did it. One of the finest and most personable officers I've worked with in a thirty-year career. Romeo was a captain of the staff, so he had a different view than Bob and I did. He was in more of a direct leadership role, doing the stuff on the ground and he delivered incredibly well. When we did go back a week later, we made sure he had clean uniform, which was a good thing, because when we arrived, I just remembering seeing him filthy and smoking cigarettes. I put him in a tough spot and he delivered. His ability to give us a framework to start from was simply amazing."

Captain Romeo Querishi in the Admin and Logistics office of the 165th tactical operations center (Romeo Qureishi's collection).

65

Inside Abu Ghraib

Back to the reconnaissance, Walters touched base with the brigade commander: "I went over and spoke with him, and he said, 'I need help with security on the perimeter, I need help on the entry control point, and I need the infrastructure brought up to acceptable standards. How soon can you be here with reinforcements to help with this and how many towers can you man on the perimeter?' I replied, 'I don't have the resources within the battalion to conduct split-based operations,' meaning, keeping some of the battalion in Balad and bringing a portion of the battalion to Abu Ghraib to meet those tasks that he gave me. I said, 'We're going to have to displace the entire battalion out of Balad and bring everybody down here. I can man three towers right now and I'll take the northern half of the perimeter wall.' He said, 'Fine. That's your call. How soon can you do it?' I said, 'We will come down here the day after Thanksgiving,' which was about a week away. That would give us the time to do a rapid tear down of everything we had up in Balad, pack everything up, pre-combat checks and inspections prior to the very large convoy of trucks, something like a hundred and thirty of them. He said, 'Thanks for your support on this.' By the end we were manning all the towers, but at this stage we simply didn't have enough soldiers with us.

"We went back, had another little huddle in front of my truck and then we convoyed back to Balad and that's when we started doing the orders process, because we have to cut an order at the battalion level for the companies, so they knew exactly what was expected of them, as far as tearing down and packing up and relocating to Abu Ghraib."

Edwards added: "After we did the leaders' recon, carried out a feel for the footprint of Abu Ghraib and headed back to Balad, it took us about five days to get all people and equipment ready. There's an operational planning piece and a logistics planning piece. The logistics was my job, to get everything together, work with the company first sergeants and sergeants major so that equipment could be loaded properly. We had to arrange for flatbed trucks through a transportation unit to carry down all our conex containers (metal shipping containers). We moved down to Abu Ghraib in serials, which are a set number of vehicles and equipment led by an officer or senior non-commissioned officer. We arranged movements into five or six serials then took the main road from Balad to Abu Ghraib driving past Taji on the way."

The arrival of the 165th certainly brought intrigue to those on site. Walters explained: "My assumption is that the detainees that were

66

inside the fenced compound and the hard stand were just seeing another U.S. Army element coming in, not knowing how long we were going to be there. They were probably just guessing what our task and purpose was going to be when we arrived. We certainly didn't share that with the detainees."

Edwards added: "When we talk about where the detainees were held, who was in charge of guarding them etc, that wasn't our mission. The detainees had no idea who we were, what we were coming to do or what our mission was. Did the units on site have an idea of why we were coming? Absolutely."

Walters explained: "The 800th Military Brigade had a military police battalion assigned to Abu Ghraib. They were in charge of everything at the time of our arrival. When we got down there, we weren't replacing another unit, we were an addition. The 165th became an additional tenant unit and we absorbed some of the responsibilities that the military police battalion had prior to our arrival. We assumed control of several of the perimeter security towers, began securing the gap in the wall and then we augmented the entry control point up front to limit access to the forward operating base. Then we assumed responsibility for infrastructure development from the military police battalion."

Neither Walters, Edwards nor the 165th had any idea just how tough and intense the next few months would prove to be. Their fundamental mission was a large task to say the least, but the environment in which they had to operate within was something they never imagined could be so severe.

9

Groundwork

"High achievement always takes place in the frame-work of high expectation."—Charles Kettering

Abu Ghraib was like walking into a minefield. Most soldiers simply weren't prepared for what lay ahead. Effective leadership was essential from the outset in order to ensure each member of personnel was equipped for the assignment which lay ahead, even when the systems may have seemed like overkill.

Assistant Operations Officer Mike Flentie explained: "We were in Germany packing up, getting ready for Iraq and there's a lot of equipment in a military property book. People were like, 'I'm not taking this. I don't need this shower tent. We're never going to use half of the stuff on this list.' There was a staff meeting and I remember LTC Walters saying, 'You will take every piece of equipment in your property book. You don't know what you are going to need or not.' People kind of laughed it off at the time, like, 'Okay, we'll take it,' but that stuck with me my whole life, because, in Abu Ghraib, we lived in a field and used every single piece of that equipment."

Walters added: "On a MTOE (Modified Table of Organizational and Equipment), which is a printout for every tactical unit in the Army, at the top of it, it has the unit's details, and underneath it would have the mission. Then under that it had a list of personnel assigned to the 165th. It's not by personnel name, it's by position. For me it would say, Battalion Commander, 05 (which was the grade of the Officer), then LTC. Then below the personnel there would be a list of all the equipment authorized for the Battalion and that equipment included things like the shower tent. The Army supply system provides that equipment and if it's destroyed in combat, they will replace it. In the same way, if we lost a member of personnel, they would also be replaced.

9. Groundwork

"So when the discussions came up, 'Sir. I don't need to take this,' I replied, 'Take everything on your property book.' I did have some experience with Desert Shield and Desert Storm eleven years earlier. We were in Saudi Arabia and we'd deployed out of Fort Bragg and didn't know how long we were going to be there. The guidance I got from my battalion commander at the time was, 'Take all your stuff and don't leave anything back, because we don't know how long this is going to last.' That was good guidance and something I was able to share with my soldiers in 2003. All we knew was that we were going to Kuwait at that point. What we didn't know was whether we were going into Iraq, so I wanted to make sure we were ready, should that eventuality occur. We also didn't know how long we might be there and where in Iraq we would be stationed. There were a lot of variables that we had no idea about, so I wanted to cover all bases."

Operation Iraqi Freedom 1 propelled thousands of U.S. soldiers into Iraq at short notice. Abu Ghraib was a monster in its own league but setting up the base in Balad acted as a good dress rehearsal. LTC Walters explained: "When we got to Balad in March 2003, it was a huge abandoned Iraqi Air Force base. The departing Iraqis had destroyed whatever they thought was of value and the rest had been ravaged by looters.

"The area we were designated to establish our tactical operation center was the site of a former air defense headquarters. We could determine that based on the air defense weapons that were outside and the ammunition that was scattered around the floor. The other side was a bakery which had a big pile of flour as tall as me dumped on the floor. Then we found another building with a bunch of chemical protective masks."

Flentie added detail at ground level: "When the war started, it was so quick. We didn't have all of our equipment yet as they were still taking it out of the port. We were sent forward to support the fight, maybe twenty-four hours after the invasion. We ended up in the middle of the desert with the tactical command post for thirty days, then moved from there to Baghdad and then up to Balad. All of our logistic trains, think of trucks, low-boys, and other vehicles bringing supplies up followed after that, maybe a couple of days after we arrived there, then the rest of our battalion joined us. I'd say maybe a third was there, possibly half.

"By the time we headed to Balad from our initial location just outside of Najaf, Baghdad had recently fallen and as we drove through it, it was a surreal experience. I was twenty-five years old at the time and we,

69

the 165th Battalion and the 205th Brigade were one of the first V Corps units to roll into Balad. This huge Air Force base was clearly deserted and was infested with aggressive feral dogs.

"We arrived in Balad late in the evening and there were very few soldiers there to provide security. That night we slept on the hoods of our Humvees and the next morning we got to work, improving perimeter security, while trying to deal with the feral dogs. We ended up at what looked like a chemical school, but it was probably just an old garrison area. We rummaged through that stuff and cleaned out all the buildings very cautiously and carefully, because we didn't know if anything had been booby-trapped. Within twenty-four hours we had already set up operations in there.

"It was pretty surreal going through these old buildings, which had a lot of anti–Iranian propaganda all over the rooms and military equipment everywhere. Balad was a key Iraqi airbase during the Iran and Iraq war. A lot of rockets were launched out of there against Iran and we ran into some of the ready rooms for the Iraqi Air Force, which had all kinds of anti–American decorations. They tried to disperse their aircrafts in the surrounding fields and at one point we even saw a MiG-31 or MiG-29 that they tried to bury, to prevent anyone else from using it.

"We set up operations fairly quickly, getting the tactical operation center ready in the hard building, with the staff in one building, the companies in others and the brigade in a building not too far away from us. Our sleeping area was in a dirt field. Pretty grim conditions.

"I came to the unit in October 2002 and had been working with LTC Walters for a few months before the deployment, then I was in Iraq for the yearlong combat tour. As for LTC Walters, I felt lucky that we had a battalion commander who had combat experience, because we were really lacking that when we started the invasion. Major Edwards joined us later in June, not long after we got there. He was the new battalion executive officer, was ready to go in this combat position and delivered to a very high standard. None of us had any idea of what Abu Ghraib was really going to be like though. We'd only heard about the horror stories from other soldiers, and they all turned out to be true."

"One last thing to add. As a unit, the 165th was never idle. Many other units may well have been. Major Edwards was neck deep in making sure the soldiers' living conditions were improved on a constant basis. Living in Balad and Abu Ghraib, I can't imagine how bad life would have been if the logistics guys hadn't been working every single hour of every day, seven days a week, to improve conditions and improve our security perimeter. There was never an idle time and the battalion leadership made sure we exercised, trained and stayed sharp. We were running five, six, seven miles a day to keep ourselves fit and many other battalions probably wouldn't have done that."

Walters paid tribute to Flentie's part in the 165th: "As with Romeo, Bill and the junior officers, Mike was in the same group. He didn't wait for me or any other senior officer to tell him how to solve the problem. He used his initiative, did a great job and that's why he went on to become a very successful officer in the Army."

◆◆◆

Having slept on Humvees for their first night in Abu Ghraib, sturdier accommodation was sought with immediate effect. Walters explained: "The military police had a morale, welfare and recreation room, but they weren't using it. We had one hundred and fifty soldiers literally stacked on top of one another who needed some space. We reached out to the military police battalion to use that room for housing soldiers and originally the military police battalion commander was okay with it, but then his operations officer went up to their military police brigade commander and complained that we were taking over their recreation room.

"The brigade commanders spoke, as one brigade commander to another. However, she was a one star general and, in the military, and when a general comes down and calls you and you're a colonel, you're going to do everything you can to appease that general officer. And if you pushed back, it got complicated."

Major Edwards added: "To me it was a no brainer. I was thinking, 'What are we talking about? Why are we even having this conversation?' In our battalion, that wouldn't have been a problem I would have brought to Bob, never mind an officer at general level. I would have made that decision myself. We had bigger things to worry about at that point. If you are bringing in a brigadier general into every conversation, then why do I need, captains, majors, lieutenants? That was madness."

Walters continued: "Normally a general officer would never be involved with that kind of decision or discussion at all. As Bill said, it was a no brainer. You had soldiers which needed a place to sleep and were under rocket fire and mortar attacks. You either put them outside exposed to that or inside under cover. For them to say, 'No. We're not sharing the room,' made no sense whatsoever.

"When my brigade commander came back to me and said, 'We're getting some push back about this room.' I said, 'Sir. Come with me.' I took him down there, showed him this totally abandoned recreation room and explained our situation. When he saw it was not being used, he was able to engage the other commander and explain that we needed soldiers sleeping inside a solid building instead of tents, in case of rocket fire or mortar attack. We ended up getting the room."

Incredibly, it seemed not everybody understood the concept of "being exposed." Edwards gave another example: "A few weeks after arriving at Abu Ghraib, the engineering units from Baghdad that were helping us lay rock, started suggesting, 'You should start looking at container housing units for your soldiers in this dirt space right here.' Bearing in mind, when I first arrived at Balad I realized our sleeping tents were unprotected from mortar round shrapnel so I drove from unit to unit on the base attempting to bargain for sandbags. The intent was to surround our sleeping areas with filled bags above the height of the cot. That would help to save lives from an exploded shell. Now, if the shell came through the top there was nothing we could do. So, here I am now being proposed with the idea of container housing units at Abu Ghraib.

"At Abu Ghraib prison there was a huge gap in the middle behind the dining facility that was just dirt. This space was about the size of a football field. Container housing units were basically little trailers that you lived in. If you had a wet unit, it meant it had a shower and a toilet. However, shower or not, we were getting indirect fire twice a day and they were suggesting we put our soldiers out in the open? The windows in the hard buildings were typically boarded up, because of mortar fire. We didn't want glass spraying all over the occupants of the building. However, if we had container housing units, windows would be the least of our worries because there would be nothing left from a direct hit.

"I replied, 'Are you absolutely crazy? No. We are staying in the prison cells where we have hard buildings surrounding us.' The container housing units never happened."

Other ingenious ideas Edwards had to contend with included explosive device architecture: "There was a fence line inside the prison and the unit before us had taken Claymore mines, which are lethal, and they had put them on the friendly side of the wire, facing inwards to the compound. The theory of the unit before us was that if they got overrun, they would use the Claymores as a defensive mechanism inside the perimeter, in essence killing everyone inside that perimeter. A completely idiotic theory. Literally one of the stupidest things I've ever seen. If you look at a Claymore, it actually says on it, 'FRONT TOWARDS ENEMY'! It was like amateur hour in preparing the defense of a military post. The leadership wasn't being involved in the decisions being made and this was yet another example of that. Let's just say those Claymores were taken off that fence very quickly when we got there."

Despite the glaring issues on arrival and a number of badly implemented standards of practice, Walters still wanted to maintain a level of decorum while making improvements: "There were other units that were tenants on the forward operating base at Abu Ghraib. The military police battalion was an example. The guidance to the 165th that I wanted implemented was, 'We want to do a good neighbor policy,' meaning, don't go in there and start changing everything just because we can. We want to work with the other tenants as a good neighbor would. It wasn't always that straight forward, but that was the thought process there."

Working off a non-existent structural backbone, Major Edwards explained the heavily loaded task of setting up the infrastructure: "When we relocated to Abu Ghraib, we moved into a place that had been occupied by multiple police battalions, a small detachment from the 205th, my brigade and the interrogation detachment that had been there. The problem was there had not been any infrastructure improvement since the military police arrived that summer.

"We had to start from the basics and establish the tactical operation center in Abu Ghraib, building everything from the core, from the inside out. We didn't have the proper wiring, doors or any walls. We were looking at the open space and saying, 'Bob's office will be in this space over there, admin will be in this part, and we will sleep over there.' The areas were separated by thin plywood walls. It was almost like we were designers. I guess, to an extent we were. At the same time, the companies in the battalion were setting up their company headquarters in the former prison cells area.

"I remember one time going over to the long-range surveillance company area and they were in a former prison section. There was a dining facility in that area which was for the prisoners in past times and all the prison spaces had solid concrete benches built into the ground, so they couldn't be moved. It was a strange place. Once, I flew in a Catholic priest from the Babylon area to put on a mass for the soldiers, which took place in that prison dining facility. When he arrived, he couldn't believe where he was about to deliver mass. That was interesting and very different."

Walters gave a small insight into the detainee setup: "They were in two different areas. One was like a big open field that was surrounded by a 14 ft. high chain fence and there was some razor wire on the top of that rolled in a concertina formation. Within that area there were hundreds of tents and the number of detainees per tent was really up to them. If they wanted a tent among themselves or have five guys in there, that was up to them, but it was all male. Whatever went on among the detainees in terms of pecking orders was largely worked out among them. The hard stand was controlled by the military police because the guard would determine which detainees went into which cells, just like you would have at a regular jail outside of a military complex.

"The food was brought in and it was like a buffet line and all the detainees were walked through that to get their food and then they were taken back to their tent and would sit outside or however they wanted to eat. They were very well nourished and the food was culturally

Detainee feeding area. Note the clothes being dried in the sun on the tents (William Edwards' collection).

appropriate. It was a contract that was set up through the military police, Combined Joint Task Force 7, providing food on a daily basis, three times a day."

With over seven thousand detainees on site, the pressure to maintain a sturdy security posture through the towers was paramount. Major Edwards recalled: "The red and yellow towers were representative of those inside the inner perimeter. These towers were manned by the military police and did not fall under our responsibility. What I found fascinating was just how makeshift the structures were. Below the towers were metal Conex storage containers that we would ship stuff over from Germany or the States, filled with equipment, but now they were being used for storage, towers, or whatever. The tops were basically plywood and 2×4 and 2×6 timber construction. Inside the plywood cavity wall they would insert sandbags in case of fire from outside the perimeter."

Walters added: "There were several guard towers around the perimeter wall of the forward operating base that the 165th were in charge of. These were permanent constructions that were built when the walls went up. Each would have a little interior staircase that went up into the

Military police overseeing the detainees (William Edwards' collection).

security tower area where the guards would stand. Up there it was open, so you could shoot your weapons if necessary.

"One of the first things we noticed when we did the initial inspection of the security towers was that the military police would have young soldiers up there for twelve hours at a time, which is not the right way to operate. I distinctly remember soon after arriving at Abu Ghraib, walking the perimeter, and going up to the guard towers with Major Mickie Williams, my sergeant major and some other leaders from our unit. There was a military police soldier up there on her own who had been there for a twelve-hour shift and didn't know what her general orders were. She had a crew-served weapon, which usually takes a couple of people to operate it effectively. The weapon was obviously in a state of neglect, was covered in dust and had not been cleaned and maintained at all. She'd never fired a weapon of this kind before, wasn't qualified to use it and didn't have any special instructions. We asked what she was doing there and she said, 'This was my shift and this is where they told me to go.' In brief, she was poorly postured to be performing her duties for security up in that tower.

Makeshift security tower overlooking detainees aimlessly walking around the compound (William Edwards' collection).

9. Groundwork

"There's three general orders when you are on guard duty and every soldier is supposed to know these. I will guard everything within the limits of my post and quit my post only when properly relieved. That's the first one. I will obey my special orders and perform my duties in a military manner. That's the second. I will report violations of my special orders, emergencies and anything not covered in my instructions to the commander of the relief. That's the third.

"The commander of the relief is typically a non-commissioned officer who would come by every so often, maybe every hour or two, to check on the soldiers. At that point the soldier would report any emergencies, or anything not stated in the special orders. Here's an example of a special order. 'You're responsible for this section. You see that tree out there, one hundred and fifty yards out? That's your left limit. And you see that house, that's your right limit. You can shoot anything in that section, but if it's outside of that, don't shoot, because it will be covered by another tower.' Something along those lines. This soldier did not know her general orders, she was there with a jug of water and she was supposed to be up there for twelve hours, which is inexplicable."

Walters continued: "We assigned towers to units. For example, the long-range surveillance company would be responsible for X number of towers and then the leadership within the long-range surveillance company would assign soldiers to pull security duty in the towers. Then they would rotate them out. Typically, there would be two soldiers up there at a time and they would be rotated every two or three hours. The non-commissioned officers would then be responsible for checking on those troops.

"The leadership would conduct spot checks of those towers to make sure they weren't up there for an inordinate amount of time, they had water, chow if they wanted it, their weapons were serviceable, and they knew their general orders and special instructions. That's some of the activity I would do on a daily basis, along with other leaders in the battalion."

◆◆◆

Being a soldier on combat deployment is a far cry from a regular 9–5 job, and time off is a concept few experienced within the 165th Battalion in Abu Ghraib. Major Edwards explained: "When we were in Balad, we were told the Army was going to start introducing a rest and recuperation program. Sergeant Major's order to the unit was,

'Whoever's been here the longest will go first and we'll start with the junior enlisted.' Bob, myself, the sergeant major, the senior people in the unit were always the last to go due to our rank and as a result we never ended up going on rest and recuperation. The location was set up near Doha, Qatar at Camp As Sayliyah and troops would get four days to relax. Also, they also were granted an exception to General Order Number One and were permitted two or three alcoholic beverages per day. Although the soldiers were allowed to go there for four days, they may be gone for seven days because transportation wasn't working or they couldn't find the right mobility unit to get them back, or whatever. It was kind of a mess.

"However, in Abu Ghraib it was a different story. There was never a day off for anyone. What we would do is ask permission to take an hour and watch an episode of something on DVD. That would be coordinated between the leadership—myself, Bob, the ops officer, the company commander, sergeant major. One of us was always in the tactical operations center.

"You have to also imagine how restricted the space was. I lived five feet from Bob, the sergeant major and our operations officer for months at a time." LTC Walters added: "Other than little periods of watching TV in your hooch, which was basically being on the other side of a piece of plywood board in the tactical operations center, there was no time off in Abu Ghraib."

A tried and tested method of successfully engaging with your fellow soldier and maintaining wellbeing is through the medium of sport. However, Abu Ghraib's facilities were far from Olympic standard. Walters explained: "I do recall back at Balad a volleyball net at some point and some of those kind of activities, but we were very limited on equipment. Ensuring that food, water, sanitation and importantly, security were in order all took priority over those relaxing activities. But as the theater grew in maturity with subsequent deployments, you would see volleyball courts set up and places where people could play softball and that kind of stuff. However, I don't recall that happening at Abu Ghraib, simply because the infrastructure was so poor, negating the possibility to do that type of activity."

Edwards added: "Runs were done in Balad. It was a really expansive airfield, with roads, sewers, sidewalks, you name it. We had the ability to exercise there and I worked out with the staff once a week. We would do a run together, which was a way for us to talk and know what was going on and stay connected. I only did it once a week because I didn't want to monopolize their time. Also, as professional officers, we expect them to take care of themselves for the other six days of the week. It's also worth noting, Balad was also open to rocket fire, so when you did exercise, you did so with caution. Here's an example why. We were trying to maintain the standard, where you took two physical fitness tests per year, one diagnostic and one for the record. We were taking a record test at Balad, when suddenly we came under mortar fire, and we had to cancel that. Bob's PT (physical training) card says, 'PT test canceled due to mortar attack.' Abu Ghraib was another level. It simply wasn't a conducive environment to exercise. Inside we did our pushups and situps, but nobody was running outside. That would have been plain stupid."

Getting to know your fellow soldier is one thing but trying to get to know the enemy was handled in a different way on site. Walters explained: "When you walked out of the tactical operations center, you were immediately in the compound where the detainees were hanging on the fences, talking and shouting at you, trying to get you to engage with them. It was a daily occurrence that you desensitized to over time.

"Most of our human intelligence collection was done based on interviews talking to detainee visitors and walk-ins as we discussed earlier. People from outside of Abu Ghraib who had family members or friends being held as detainees would come to the visitor center, which was basically an empty building, with some tables and chairs in it. They would wait for the military police to escort the detainees over and then return after. That's how our human intelligence collection was going on in the vicinity of Abu Ghraib in addition to the long-range surveillance missions."

While physical exercise within the walled boundaries of Abu Ghraib was risky, the immediate surrounding area was no holiday destination. Majors Edwards explained why: "Abu Ghraib was in the heart of what was known as the Sunni Triangle—a notoriously dangerous placement on the map. The northern tip is Tikrit, the lower eastern point is Baghdad and the western mark is Ramadi. The midway point between Ramadi and Baghdad is Fallujah, and Abu Ghraib is located between Fallujah and Baghdad. Any places smaller than that in the surrounding area wouldn't have hit my radar, unless we went there for a specific long-range surveillance mission or something to that effect.

"Whenever Romeo and I sent Muhamed and Amar out, we never told them where to go. They went to wherever to find what we needed and had free movement. I didn't travel with those guys at all, because that would have been very dangerous. And if we left the forward operating base and were returning, the locals in that area who were guiding us would know where to lead us. We had to be very careful. What we would do when coming up to the entry control point, is dismount and walk alongside the trucks, because we'd have Iraqi locals coming up to the truck trying to sell us stuff. What we didn't want was somebody coming up to the truck with a grenade or an explosive, or something of that nature. Walking alongside was really smart to do, because, inside the truck, you don't have as much maneuverability if a threat came towards you."

Walters added. "Typically, when we rolled out of the base at Abu Ghraib, we had a destination that we were headed to and there was no deviation from that. The destination was briefed prior to going out. You would have to get the mission approved before leaving the compound. It would be briefed to the leadership, they would approve it and that was generally done at the operations officer level. It would have to be a more sensitive mission for it to come up to me for approval. Maybe some type of surveillance mission in Fallujah or something like that.

"After rolling out of the tactical command center, they would call the center on the radio and say, 'This convoy is exiting now, heading towards Baghdad International Airport for example. They would go from the forward operating base to their destination, keeping us posted until they arrived there. Likewise on the way back. Stopping along the way to shop on the local economy to get basic supplies was absolutely not acceptable."

Getting used to the rustic surroundings of Abu Ghraib took the 165th by surprise. The levels of grime, vermin and danger made it memorable for all the wrong reasons.

10

Beyond the Pale

"We finally nestled in at Balad and made a little life for ourselves and it kind of got comfortable, then we get a call to go to Abu Ghraib. It was a shithole in a terrible area. Nobody was happy about it. My initial impressions were 'catastrophe.' As bad as the living conditions were at Balad, Abu Ghraib was horrible. People today going to Iraq and Afghanistan have facilities, dining areas, we had nothing. We basically lived in a field and slept in tents that sometimes were over one hundred degrees. You try and sleep in that temperature with mice everywhere."
—Mike Flentie, Assistant Operations Officer

When you mention Abu Ghraib to anyone, the first thing they tend to think of is the detainee abuse. The revelations were shocking and the photos which flooded the global media frontpages were sickening. However, there's another abhorrent side to Abu Ghraib that many never knew about and only the soldiers deployed there could empathize with. LTC Walters and Major Edwards—with almost seventy years of military experience between them—helped to shine a torch into a few murky corners at Abu Ghraib.

Major Edwards voiced his recollections: "I'd been to Kuwait setting up Kabals in the late 1990s out in the desert doing a lot of training and having a lot of downtime. That was my experience of the Middle East at that point, and it was a good one. As a comparison, Abu Ghraib was hell on earth. It was the absolute worst, horrific place I've ever been on this planet. It looked like something from an apocalyptic movie.

"The place smelled really foul. When you have over seven thousand detainees right there inside the fenced compound and the rest of the infrastructure had not been brought up to respectable standards, that's what happens. I'm not talking about the standard of the home I live in at present, I'm talking about an acceptable military standard for a grim environment, meaning you have field sanitation in place or you don't have disease wiping out formations."

LTC Walters concurred: "In addition to the sanitation issues, from my experience in Iraq, Afghanistan and some of the other Middle East locations I've been to, the volume of activity was much higher in Abu Ghraib than anywhere else. When it came to the number of encounters with the enemy, whether it be them shooting at us, indirect fire from mortars or rockets, attacking our security towers, shooting at the entry control point, Abu Ghraib was in a league of its own. Every evening, especially when the sun went down, we would get hit with mortars."

Edwards added: "Most of the mortars and rockets that came in were former Iraqi Army ammunitions, most of which were Russian manufactured, although Chinese 107mm rockets were also prevalent as were Iranian munitions. We were able to identify this, based on the remnants post attack. We'd go out, take pictures of where the mortars had detonated inside the compound and typically, for the rockets especially, you'd find tail fins that were used to stabilize the ammunition when it was shot from the point of origin to the point of impact. Once it had been detonated, typically, the fins were not consumed in the explosion, so you could identify the caliber and the manufacturer.

"Later on, as the U.S. Army matured, I was deployed with what was called a weapons intelligence team. We would do post attack forensics. This was in the 2009–2011 time period. But during Abu Ghraib, we weren't as mature in that capability, so simply taking pictures and then annotating the point of impact is really all you could do."

Walters explained the firepower available on site to counter these attacks: "There was a minimum level of ammunition stock, which was called a 'basic load' and each company had an ammunition storage area. Every soldier had their personal assigned weapon. For me, it was a Beretta 9mm side arm, which was typical of what the more senior officers carried. More junior soldiers typically had a 5.56mm automatic rifle such as an M4 or M16. In addition to that, you had a certain number of crew-served weapons. Within the long-range surveillance company, you typically had the squad automatic weapon, which was a machine gun, then you also had the 50 caliber crew-served weapons which we had mounted on our vehicles. You also had AT4s, which are anti-tank rockets. The towers would either have an automatic weapon or a 7.62mm, typically an M60 machine gun. Essentially, there was plenty of firepower to protect the base, which in the case of Abu Ghraib was more than a necessity.

"By the time I'd got to Abu Ghraib, I'd become a more senior officer. For example, my most recent deployment, I was a two-star general in Afghanistan. I wasn't kicking in doors or anything like that, I was working in a headquarters building. Unless the headquarters gets hit with rocket fire or something like that, you're just not as exposed to the enemy as when you're at a lower level. At Abu Ghraib, it didn't discriminate your rank. Everybody was exposed to continuous incoming fire at any given time."

◆◆◆

Sanitation conditions were far from desirable. Edwards explained: "In terms of sewage systems, functioning pipes or anything like that, there wasn't any. When we got to Abu Ghraib, there was a tremendous lack of Porta Potties initially, so we used our own 'burnouts.' These were fifty-gallon drums cut in halves or quarters that would be slid under a piece of wood with a hole in it. That's where you went to the bathroom. The way you did a burnout was pulling out the fifty gallon can with all the excrement inside, pouring diesel fuel on it and setting fire to it. You'd then push the can back under the wooden toilet and that was that. We had burn sessions throughout the day, normally one in the morning, afternoon and one in the evening. Very basic, but effective.

"We also had these big white PVC tubes about four or five inches wide and the engineers would take these pipes and drill them into the ground, and we would pee into the earth," Walters added. "The technical term was 'Piss tube!'"

Edwards laughed, adding: "We also had burnouts in Balad and people would time the burn sessions to when they knew when the cans were going to be cleaned. Then you'd see this mad comical dash towards the toilets with everyone carrying their toilet paper.

"At Abu Ghraib, when we first got there, the Porta Potties were under a bad contract, which meant the units weren't being serviced. You can imagine, these things were full to capacity and overflowing. Unsanitary was certainly an accurate term. So what me and Romeo did was get a new contractor set up for the battalion to have more Porta Potties and also to have them serviced twice a day.

"Getting the Porta Potties after about a month was a serious luxury. However, when the detainees and some of our workers who were locally

The original portable toilets at Abu Ghraib. Hardly state of the art but did the job (William Edwards' collection).

sourced went to the bathroom, they wouldn't sit on the Porta Potti, they would stand and hover above it. Let's just say it was always really nasty in there. The disposal from the bathrooms was not sanitary disposal, it was just waste disposal as the contract allowed. Between the smell of human waste, the body odour and this sea of people that were living in these wretched conditions, the place smelled horribly and that smell stayed with you the entire time you were there."

Each soldier had an allocation of about three to four sets of uniform, so laundry was an essential part of the daily practice, as was hygiene. Walters explained: "One of the things we emphasized as part of the deployment was sanitation and personal hygiene. When you do that, you minimize illness. Brush your teeth, clean your feet, do those things to keep yourself clean. We tried to up the standards wherever we went. When we got to Abu Ghraib we were starting from the most horrific standards and all the measures we took were simply to try and take it up to a liveable standard.

"My daily routine was to go out to the water buffalo, which was a trailer behind a truck that had a five-hundred-gallon tank. That's where

10. Beyond the Pale

Inside Abu Ghraib. If only you could add smell to photos (William Edwards' collection).

we stored our water. I had my pink, plastic washbasin, which was about two feet in diameter, around eight inches deep and held about a gallon of water. The guys all used to tease me about the color of my washbasin, and I used to tell them, 'At least nobody will try and steal it.' Once I got to the water buffalo, I'd fill it with water and the temperature of the day basically reflected the temperature of the water. Hot water in June, cold water in December. I would then take my washbasin back and I would shave in the bucket, wash my face and head and I would strip down, stand in the bucket and wash my body.

"The detainees would do their laundry in buckets of water and hang them up on the tent and leave the sun to dry them. That may sound like a tough way to do it, but we also did our laundry ourselves. Instead of putting the clothes up on the roof of the tent though, we would string up a clothesline. That's how you washed your clothes at Abu Ghraib. After laundry, I'd get dressed and proceed with the day's activities."

Edwards added: "Everyone had their own personal routines. I would ask Dana to send me vitamins. We were fortunate to not have a mass outbreak of any kind of illness, but soldiers did get sick. I got strep throat when I was at Abu Ghraib, but I went to the medical tent, got some antibiotics and it was gone within 48 hours. If something was really bad, we had the capability to MEDEVAC somebody out of there.

"In terms of the water buffalo. You could bathe in that water, but you'd try not to get it in your mouth as it was not drinkable. When it came to laundry, I had a little washboard to scrub my clothes. The moment I put my clothes in the water and started to scrub, the water would turn black right away. Then I'd hang them up and in the heat, they'd be dry in a couple of minutes."

With unsanitary conditions came unwanted guests. Major Edwards shared his experiences: "From the moment you landed in Iraq, there were smells and the air quality wasn't great. You start getting used to it, but it was horrible. Even to this day, if I get a distinct smell of wood burning, it will flash me back to that type of aroma in Abu Ghraib.

"When we came out to Iraq in the summer of 2003, the temperatures were hot. You were hovering around 130 Fahrenheit on certain days. Then as you transition into the fall you start to get cooler weather and the smells started to change with the weather. When the temperature dropped to 90, it felt like you were freezing because of the comparison to the summer temperature. When we moved into the fall, from the November to February timeframes, we were all wearing jackets and it wasn't actually that cold. It was just the drastic change.

"If you look at the photos you can see the ground is wet, because it was wintertime when we arrived. There was a smell of mud, sewage and dirt from all the pools of water, so one of my first tasks was contracting guys to bring in gravel and spread it over the pools to absorb some of that water, because wherever you had standing water you had the possibility of waterborne insects and disease. The last thing we needed was to have a bunch of soldiers and detainees getting sick and dying from dysentery or what have you.

"Although we were in a malaria zone, I don't remember anyone contracting the disease while we were there. We had malaria pills that we took on a daily basis. You got up in the morning you did your personal hygiene regimen and then you would take your malaria pills along with your vitamins and whatever else you had. I think the system served us well."

While the female Anopheles mosquito didn't make its mark with malaria, a rather larger and thirstier character certainly left a lasting impression at Abu Ghraib. Major Edwards explained. "We had an issue with camel spiders. They were about six inches long, were attracted to any source of water and look nasty and prehistoric. When we first got to Abu Ghraib, we didn't have showers set up, but after a few weeks I asked our contractors, Muhamed and Amar, to organize for showers to be built. They went to Baghdad, bought a miniature water heater, hooked it up to the water buffalo, then ran a hose out from it into the plywood shower area.

"When we finally got this thing built, I would shower in my running shoes. Before you went in, you had to check for camel spiders, because if there was any sort of dampness or water they congregate to that point. You might have fifteen to twenty of them in one place and they're massive and hard to kill. They'll actually come at you. Perhaps not you as the person, but certainly as a result of them seeing a shadow, a light source or in this instance water."

Higher up in the food chain and far more destructive were rodents. Major Edwards recalled: "When we were out in Ramadi with the long-range surveillance guys, we were on the river Euphrates. The rats along that river were huge and we would see them all the time. Then when we were in Balad we were occupying these cinderblock mud buildings, which had holes in the walls that were accessible from the outside. That led to a serious mouse issue. I asked Amar and Muhamed and this Kurdish kid to go into the towns and cities to get traps. They came back with suitable contraptions for Euphrates and Tigris river rats. These traps were bigger than a shoebox. I remember saying to Amar, 'I'm looking to stop mice, not rats.' He said, 'We don't have those sort of traps here.'

"In Balad I had a box of snack bars that someone had sent me. I had to make a little pulley system in my living area, so I could hang the box from the roof. If I left it on the floor, the mice would get in and eat all the snacks. I learned my lesson, hung it from the roof of the building, but then I found they were climbing up the string that I had rigged it with. These were ranger qualified mice in Iraq!

"I got a hold of my dad and he managed to send me around a hundred mouse traps about a month later and I shared them around the unit. I'm not kidding—I set up two traps in my little sleeping space, turned off the light and within a minute both traps snapped."

"Then we got to Abu Ghraib and we still had the rodent issue. I would set my traps and take the peanut butter from the 'meals ready to eat' (MREs) and put a little on the mouse trap and set them out, then turn off the lights. Within a minute, you'd hear them snap and I'd catch two mice. Snap, snap. I'd go and pick them up, throw them away and then set the traps again and the same thing. Snap, snap. It was like a game, which never stopped."

Far from tranquil, it was no surprise that sleeping patterns for soldiers in Abu Ghraib were testing. Edwards explained: "Trying to sleep in Abu Ghraib was a rollercoaster. I don't think I've recovered. In my instance, I would try to sleep when it was appropriate. The sleep patterns were maybe three or four hours and then you may be up doing something, then taking a little break later, something like a twenty or thirty-minute power nap. There was no consistency. It was a case of sleep when you can and try to keep your body healthy. For me, I did that by doing things like pushups and sit ups, eating the best I could. Later on in my career, I heard the Chief of Staff Army talk one time, who was our senior Army commanders and he said, 'As a leader, you should do four things. Sleep, read, eat and stay physically active.'

Walters added: "In order to be deployed for a year you had to rest. It's a different type of resting to when you are not deployed. My sleeping was more situationally dependent. For example, if we were inserting a unit on a patrol, I would typically stay awake until the insertion was complete. Simply because if something was going to happen it would be at the infiltration or exfiltration. Once they were in, around 11pm or so, I'd try to get some sleep.

"Typically, I've always been an early riser and would always try and do personal hygiene, some exercise and then start the day, getting up at about 5 a.m. If I could get five hours of sleep in a night, that was a good night, but it was rare you'd have more than a night or two that it would happen, because things would occur, and as leaders you responded to those things. What's good about the team we had was that if I wasn't there, Bill would take over and issue the appropriate orders or if we were both gone, the operations officer would. There was never a point when all of the senior grades were gone. We would always keep one of them in the tactical operations center to deal with emerging events."

Sleeping patterns and personal hygiene are heavily influenced by the external environment. Walters explained: "In addition to the fluctuation of temperature, dust storms were also an issue in Iraq. Not so much during the winter, but in the spring and summer we had some severe storms which were like a wall of sand that you could see approaching, which was amazing to see. When it hit you, everything turned orange and if you put your hand in front of you, it was difficult to see your fingers. We had this breakfast drink called Tang, which the astronauts used. It's a powder which you would mix with water and it turned into an orange flavored drink. When you stepped out of your vehicle, or tent and this storm was upon you, everything was orange, like Tang."

Referring to the photo of the two soldiers from 165th sitting in their chairs as the sandstorm was in motion, Walters added a little extra color to the scene: "If you look behind them, that is a burnout. They were probably on burnout duty at the moment that photo was taken. The soldiers might have slid out those wooden plywood flaps and pulled out those buckets to burn the human waste. I'm guessing that's what they were doing, because nobody would sit and relax next to a burnout unless they had to!"

While the 165th was acclimating to its new environment, the families back in Germany also had their challenges.

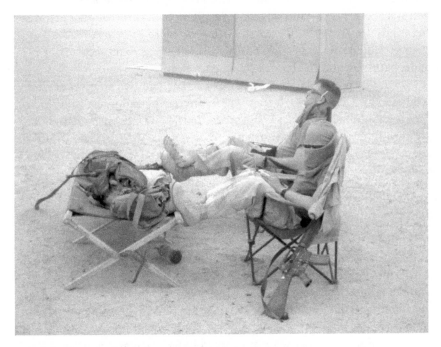

Soldiers relaxing during a sandstorm, next to burnouts (Robert Walters' collection).

11

Resident Nightingale

"The miracle is not that we do this work, but that we are happy to do it."—Mother Teresa

Informing families of the constantly evolving situation was an essential part of Nancy's role as the wife of a deployed battalion commander on the post in Darmstadt, however, her responsibilities and actions went far beyond. Nancy recalled two very tough episodes: "Around November 2003, after both girls were back in the U.S. with their grandparents, the losses really started having an impact on our brigade, battalion and the base support battalion.

"On one particular occasion, our brigade had two soldiers severely wounded and even though they weren't in our battalion we went to see how we could help. I took two awesome battle buddies with me to Landstuhl which was a two-hour drive from where we were in Darmstadt, to see what was happening for these soldiers and to see if there was anything we could do. One of the first things we saw after the soldiers were MEDEVACed, was that they didn't have anything with them. No money, no phonecards, nothing to read, no change of clothes, just whatever the U.S. military hospital at Landstuhl could provide. These were not a major priority, but things that needed to be addressed.

"There were also two soldiers in ICU that were induced into medical comas because their wounds were very severe. It was late at night and the father of one of the soldiers was being flown in. He was a professor in either Saudi or Kuwait. His wife didn't want to come because she didn't want to say, 'Pull the plug on my son.' The father connected with us because we were people not dressed in uniform and were just family members like him. He grabbed onto us pretty tightly. His son was in bad shape, but the other soldier was in worse shape. Really bad. He was in a room where the temperature was kept very cold and because these soldiers had been sitting down when the blast came into their tent, it took out their gut area. They had just done surgery, but couldn't close this particular soldier.

"We had the TV on and we were whispering in his ear, not knowing if he could hear us or not. They told me that they weren't sure when his mom was going to get there as they were trying to put together the necessary requirements to get her over from the United States, because they didn't know if he was going to live or even make the trip to Walter Reed (National Military Medical Center in D.C.).

"The next day, one of Bob's rear detachment, senior non-commissioned officers, one of the battle buddies from the night before, went back with me to the hospital, because we were hoping to be there before the mother arrived from the U.S. We wanted another 'mom' standing there with her. We had left really early from Darmstadt, but when we came down the hospital hallway we saw that the staff had to help her walk because when she saw her son, she lost the feeling in her legs.

"She came and sat with me at the back of a waiting room. By now, there was a lot of people in there from the unit trying to help. We found out that she had taken the initiative and made it to Germany on her own. She didn't have her passport or any documents, but somehow had made it to the point of her son's bed. She gave all the credit to God. She had never flown before. Her church and the local community gave her the money to go right away. I remember laughing with her because being post 9/11, God was the only one who could make that possible.

"Later that day, she and I were talking and she asked if we would pray with her, for her son, and the father of the other soldier asked if we would pray for his son, which we most certainly did. A problem then arose because the Air Force wasn't going to let the mom get on the plane to Walter Reed with her son. The point is that the family member flies with the injured party in case something happens on the flight. If the member passed away, they would be there with them. They weren't going to let her on though because she had no documentation.

"I told the unit that I would buy us both tickets and I'd fly with her. There was no way this mom was going to fly alone after seeing the shape her son was in. That night I was sitting on the floor in the hallway of the ICU and was trying to rest a little bit, when the mom came running out, because the plane had just arrived with all the personal effects of both soldiers. The mom came running out to me, because her son's Bible was there and she was so excited, because he had folded down pages and had written and made notes in the margin of what 'Mom was trying to teach me.'

"She was clinging to that Bible for dear life and was sitting on the floor next to me crying. It was about 2 am by now. Then the rear detachment brigade non-commissioned officer came up to me with his radio and said, 'I've got your husband on the phone.' The moment I heard Bob's voice, I started crying. He said, 'Sweetheart. Did he get his Bible?' I said, 'Yes. His mother has it with her and is with me right now.' He said, 'That's all he kept screaming, 'I want my Bible." Then the phone went dead. I had no idea how Bob was involved in that particular situation.

"The Air Force did eventually get the mom on the plane and flew her to Walter Reed with her son. It was maybe about a month or so later I was sitting in a briefing, finding out what was happening to the different units, losses and wounded, when a soldier walked in and said there was a message that he wanted to pass on to me. I assumed it was from Bob, but it was actually from Walter Reed, letting me know that both of those soldiers had woken up. Not only had they woken up, but they were very hungry and wanted to go back to the fight to be with their brothers and sisters in the war. One of them was able to go back to active duty and one was not. It was a miracle they were both even alive."

When news of tragedy surfaced from a deployment, the aftermath always remained the same. Thankfully, neither LTC Walters or Major Edwards wives ever got "that" knock on the door. However they were immersed into the slipstream of the other families' loss at the base. Nancy explained: "I was devastated for the families directly affected since their worlds were shattered. At the same time, you feel guilty for being relieved the knock did not come to your door this time. Throughout my husband's commands, spouses had requested that I be included immediately after they had been notified of their soldier's death. I had to do that one time, a few years later, when Bob had become Brigade Commander. I got a call about a spouse whose husband was in a different unit. She was the family readiness group liaison for one of our battalions and a friend to many of us.

"Her husband had been on the ground in Afghanistan for just a few weeks and was killed. I got a call that she had requested for me and another spouse to be there. That other spouse was also one of the battle buddies in Germany that had gone to Landstuhl with me. We found ourselves riding again together to another tragic situation. The chaplain was there, and soldiers were also there to support and help her with all the paperwork. She had one little girl who was six years old.

"The spouse was standing at the end of her driveway with a trash bag, waiting for us to get there. When we got out of the car, she explained the reason she was carrying around the trash bag. The last night before her husband went on deployment, she would take the pillow cases and sheets, not wash them and keep them in a trash bag, so that when she missed him, she could pull out a pillowcase and smell his sweat or his cologne. She said, 'They're trying to take my trash bag away. Don't let them take it.' That trash bag was more valuable than gold to her.

"When I walked into the house, her little daughter said to me, 'They told me my daddy's not coming home.' I said, 'I know baby.' They had a counselor and a doctor there also. She was drawing a picture of a rainbow, with her daddy above the rainbow and was trying to draw a picture of what she thought Jesus looked like to her.' She said, 'My daddy can see the top of the rainbows now,' and I said, 'Yes, he can.'

"Every few minutes she would then say, 'But I want him to come home.' I'd say, 'I know. I know.' You're supposed to let them deal with it, in relation to their age and some of the things they say is heart wrenching. She'd then say, 'He needs to just come back home.' All I could say was, 'I know.'

"These are episodes you never forget."

12

Managing Death

"Those who have long enjoyed such privileges as we enjoy, forget in time that men have died to win them."
—Franklin D. Roosevelt

Contrary to how war is portrayed through the soft-focus lens of a Hollywood camera, the reality is that when a soldier is lost in combat, ticker tape parades are the last thought on anyone's mind in the battalion. Death is a harsh reality for anybody on combat deployment. LTC Walters explained: "When you're in a combat zone, it doesn't matter where you are at, you're going to encounter death. Depending on the echelon, you're going to see it up close and it's devastating when that happens."

Major Edwards recalled his first encounter with death in the military: "I was a young Lieutenant stationed in Germany at the time and one of our soldiers was killed in an accident that required a 15–6 investigation [the commander's tool to get facts on any situation they deem necessary. It is not punitive but rather a tool that provides for decision making]. However, Iraq in 2003 is where I first saw a dead person from a war combat zone. I was thirty-two at the time.

"Seeing a dead body for the first time, it's surreal and strange. Then, when it happens again, you get a little bit more desensitized to it, especially during that time period of 03/04 in Abu Ghraib. It was literally the Wild West. The long-range surveillance guys would bring a dead combatant back to the forward operating base or there would be a death from an engagement we were in. Whatever it was, you simply had to focus on the mission, your teammates and move on. You're in a combat zone and emotionally, everyone expects to see something like that. Regardless, it affects you as a person. It is never easy."

Edwards recalled one particular episode which is deeply ingrained in his heart: "I was a reserve officers' training corps instructor at the University of Tennessee from 1999–2002 at the time. One of the cadets I brought into the program really stood out. The story behind this kid is great. He wasn't a great high school student. He had a 2.0 GPA, a 19 on his ACT, so all the bare minimums.

"He was from a town in Tennessee and one day drove up with his father to Knoxville where I was at and explained that all he wanted to do all his life was be an Army officer. However, with his academic record, there was no way I could get this kid into the University of Tennessee. Well, I didn't think I could.

"I went to my boss at the time and said, 'I'd really like to take a chance on this guy. I really like him.' He said, 'Go to the admissions office and see if you can talk them into allowing him into the University.' I went over the admissions and he said, 'Okay. Let's get him in and give him a chance.'

"This guy comes in and does amazing school work his first semester. Goes on to graduate, becomes an infantry officer, goes to ranger school and does what he set out to do. Then I heard around 2006/7, he was killed in combat in Baghdad. That hit me kind of hard."

Walters recalled his experience of death on the battlefield: "For me, the first time was Desert Shield and Desert Storm. It was in January of 1991, and it was Iraqi soldiers that had been killed when we attacked going into Kuwait. I'd just turned thirty years of age. From my perspective, the experience caught me off guard. What happened was, we came up on an Iraqi position that had been hit by artillery fire and I don't know what I was expecting, but I wasn't expecting to see Iraqi bodies left inside this position. I was a company commander at the time and I was asked, 'What do we do?,' and I said, 'Let's focus on the mission. Let's do that.' I had to shift the narrative from, here's the dead guys to, what are we supposed to be doing and what's our purpose? I tried not to dwell on the situation and also wanted the soldiers to do the same and focus on something positive.

"When we came across those bodies, we didn't go through them, because we were not around at the time of their death, which meant we didn't know if the enemy had boobytrapped them. We were in a movement at that point and had to Charlie Mike. We made notification to our higher headquarters of the location, what we'd seen there and then moved out.

"Just to add, as far as enemy death goes, if there were troops in

95

contact and a long-range surveillance soldier had killed an enemy insurgent, here's what would typically happen. If the proximity to the body and the area was secure, i.e., there's no gunfire going on, the procedure was to search the fallen adversary, take any weapons they have on them and search their pockets for anything that could be of intel value. Then you leave the body there. One time we had the long-range surveillance team make a mistake and bring a body back to the headquarters in Balad and then as soon as they brought it in, I said, 'Hey guys. You've got to take it back, so the body can be claimed by the Iraqi family, who lost their loved one.' That's what we did the next day. We did a combat mission, got him out there and returned the body to the family. That's how it typically happened, but a lot of times though, insurgents, if they have somebody shot, wounded or killed, they would drag them off themselves and it didn't become an issue, but otherwise, those were the procedures at the time."

Fast forward to early fall of 2003, Walters recalled the first casualty they experienced in Balad: "The soldier was an augmentee from a sister battalion which was assigned to the 205th Brigade and was also a tenant unit in Balad. He was a cook and was coming back on a logistics convoy from Baghdad, up Main Supply Route, Tampa, coming towards Balad.

"While driving up Main Supply Route, Tampa, they were hit by an IED just north of Baghdad. During that time, we didn't have any up-Armored vehicles. They were all soft skin, meaning they were either canvas or nothing. In addition, they had no doors. So when that IED went off, it was a catastrophic kill. It destroyed the vehicle, wounded some of the soldiers inside and killed the augmentee closest to the blast.

"I joined the quick reaction force team that was mainly manned with our long-range surveillance personnel. We went down to the site of the ambush that day and there were some materials still in the vehicle, including a large piece of metal shrapnel about six inches long and two inches wide. One of the soldiers there who helped the MEDEVAC had the soldier's wallet for some unknown reason and he handed it to me because of my rank."

Assistant Operations Officer Mike Flentie recalled: "We'd been hit by an IED and our battalion had to go and recover the vehicle and bring it back. The memory that is ingrained in my mind is seeing LTC Walters walking back from the motor pool with the bloody wallet of the soldier that was killed in the Humvee and the look of anger and sadness on his face. Something that will stick with me forever."

12. Managing Death

Walters continued: "When I got back to Balad I went to brief the 205th brigade commander. I showed him the type of shrapnel I discovered at the ambush site. It was a piece of a 152mm artillery shell from the Iraqi Army. The purpose of bringing that back was to show the leadership in the brigade what the enemy was doing and that they had got hold of Iraqi ammunition and were using them against coalition forces. They took this artillery round and then put additional explosives and a triggering device on it and set it off when a convoy went by."

Edwards added: "The shocking thing to all of us was holding this piece of metal and thinking, 'When this things goes off and goes through the air, there's no way you're surviving.' Shortly after this attack, I went on the mission of up Armoring all of our trucks. We didn't have the necessary equipment, so we set up a welding shop in the maintenance area and rolled the vehicles in one by one. We put sandbags on the floor and I started acquiring steel. Visualize sparks flying as we started welding doors, gun turrets and mounts in mass production in the maintenance space, until every truck we could up Armor was covered. I got some comments from a sister battalion executive officer that I'd ruin the suspension on the vehicles and I said, 'Then let's get heavier shock absorbers!' We had to get really reactive once the enemy changed tactics. There was no other option. They changed tactics, we changed tactics."

◆◆◆

On October 6, 2003, Specialist Karol, from Woodruff, Arizona, was killed near Hit, Iraq. The soldier who was stationed out of Darmstadt, Germany was only 20 years old. LTC Walters expanded on the details of that fateful night and the process of managing the passing of a fallen soldier. "Specialist Karol was in a civilian sport utility vehicle and was going to do an insertion of a long-range surveillance team at night. The reason they were in this type of vehicle is so the enemy would not know there were U.S. soldiers inside, which in turn would minimize ambush risk. That night, Specialist Karol, who was one of the junior guys on the team, was in the back of the SUV when they left the hard paved road and started driving over the sand. That's when they ran over a landmine.

"That mine exploded right beneath specialist Karol and he was killed instantly. The vehicle flipped over and all the soldiers were rattled. They then had to assess their situation, call in the mine strike and establish security, which is always the first priority. They established security and communications, reporting that there were other soldiers who were shaken up and wounded and then there was their team member who was dead and there was absolutely nothing they could do for him.

"I flew out the next day to Al Asad airbase. The company commander was out there, and the soldiers were traumatized, because they'd had this young soldier on their team for quite a while and to have him killed in front of you is very emotionally challenging. What you have to do as leaders is focus the soldiers on something positive. I told the battalion, 'You focus on the mission. The mission doesn't stop because you lose a soldier, the mission's going to continue.'

"Whenever there is a situation like this, you need to tell them the things they've been doing well and some things they can improve on, but you also remember the soldier that you lost, by having a ceremony and recognizing him. The leader and chaplain will speak at that ceremony, followed by the soldier's friends. They'll have a memorial there with the boots, a rifle turned upside down, his ID tags, a helmet and sometimes a picture if we had one. Some people would go over and lay down unit coins at the boots. Then all the soldiers would go through, pay their respects, talk about what's happened amongst themselves and then disperse.

"At the end of the memorial, the Sergeant Major would do a roll call. Here's how that worked. Let's say there were five soldiers on that long-range surveillance team that night, the Sergeant Major would say 'Specialist Jones' for example. Specialist Jones will shout, 'Here Sergeant Major.' Then say, 'Specialist Smith,' and he would shout, 'Here Sergeant Major.' He'd then do the same with the other two officers and then he'd say, 'Specialist Karol.' And there would be nothing. Silence. Then he would say 'Specialist Spencer Karol,' and again, still silent. Then he'd say 'Specialist Spencer T. Karol,' and once again it was silent. It's a very solemn ceremony as you can imagine. At the end of the silence after the roll call and no response from Specialist Karol, at that point it goes to 'Taps,' which is the song which is played by a bugle when we have a fallen comrade.

"While all of this is happening, you have next of kin notification occurring. Units back in the States or Germany are tasked to provide casualty assistance officers, who will go to the family and notify them, when they've lost a loved one. For Specialist Karol, it was a challenge because his parents were divorced and lived in different places. We had to ensure that both mother and father, who were his next of kin were notified as close to the exact same time as possible. That had to occur before any word of specialist Karol being killed and disseminated between the company or the battalion. We didn't want the family members who had just lost their son to find out in a newspaper article or on the TV that they no longer had a son.

"These next of kin notification teams show up in dress uniform and will typically be an officer, a senior non-commissioned officer and chaplain. You hear these stories about family members just collapsing in tears when they get that knock at the door and there's three guys standing there in dress uniform. They know what that means.

"That's how we dealt with death on the battlefield. You have a ceremony, a dignified transfer of the remains on to a U.S. Air Force aircraft with an escort from the soldier's unit to ensure a dignified transfer, then that aircraft will fly the remains, which are processed in Dover, Delaware. The soldier, in their dress uniform with all their appropriate medals or awards that they earned while they served, would then have another dignified transfer to where the family wants to bury their loved one. We call that, the hero's flight.

"There would then be a military funeral conducted at that location. Typically, there would be volleys of fire as a part of the Taps ceremony and then the senior officer or non-commissioned officer would present a folded flag that had been draped over the coffin to the next of kin."

Edwards: "Listening to Bob's perspective as battalion commander, it was so critical in getting those things right he mentioned. Focusing on the mission, doing a quick after action review. These are the things you're doing good, these are the things you can improve on.

"On the other side, when Specialist Karol was killed, my role as the executive officer in the unit was to make sure all those logistic pieces were happening that Bob was describing. I think I was up for thirty-six hours after Specialist Karol was killed, because I was with some key staff coordinating with casualty assistance. I was personally able to talk to mortuary affairs, to make sure everything was right and on the other side coordinating escorts for the soldier back to the homeland.

"It was a very intense period. One moment we were taking a combat patrol brief, the next moment we were dealing with casualties and the next, day to day functions. It was a pretty traumatic event for the unit. We had a part in the memorial that Bob spoke about. We also did a memorial in Balad in the hangar at the airport and there was a big showing from supporting units. The backside support that goes into making a logistic event as professional as possible that all the i's are dotted and t's are crossed, is a very large task.

"At that point you're trying to keep the battalion focused on the mission so there's not a sense of revenge or something like that. When it's a personal friend or someone close to them, the natural instinct is to respond in a certain way, so, part of leadership is to make sure that we keep their focus on the unit's task and purpose."

A few months after the passing of Specialist Karol, a fitting tribute was made in his honor at Abu Ghraib. Edwards explained: "When we were in Balad, we had a range on the forward operating base that we could go to, in order to maintain our marksmanship skills and keep our proficiency up. After getting the security and infrastructure up to speed at Abu Ghraib, the guys wanted to have a range where they could stay proficient. They also wanted to dedicate the range to specialist Karol. There were two buildings in the northeast corner of Abu Ghraib that were unoccupied. These were buildings that at one point were used by the Iraqis in the past, but were uninhabitable from our perspective. That's where I decided the range would go, between the two buildings.

Karol Range plaque at Abu Ghraib range (William Edwards' collection).

"At the time we had an engineer unit that was tasked by the V Corps to help us with infrastructure, dispersing gravel and similar tasks. They came in with bulldozers and other machinery, moving earth all around in between these two buildings, to build a really large mound to stop ammunition going through the perimeter wall and into the countryside or local villages. We put about five or six firing positions in the range, which was used on a frequent basis.

"Either the base mayor or Romeo sent Muhamed or Amar into one of the cities and got them to make a golden plaque with the name of the range. 'Dedicated in memory of Specialist Spencer Timothy Karol, 2nd Platoon, Echo Company, 51st Infantry Regiment.' We had the plaque mounted on one of the buildings. When we left Abu Ghraib, we handed the range over to the 203rd and they were thankful to have 'Karol Range.'"

The stark reality of death was never far away in Abu Ghraib, but day to day operations still needed to continue and the infrastructure was far from complete. The challenges of sourcing the appropriate equipment and labor to complete the tasks was far from easy.

13

Locally Sourced

"Battles, unlike bargains, are rarely discussed in society."—James Fenimore Cooper

When you are tasked with converting a field full of rubble, ruins, human remains and vermin into a functioning area, you need to be somewhat resourceful. Being in tune with the population on your doorstep, getting to grips with the local economy and providing a taste of home are all essential in trying to keep the soldiers' morale up. However, without a stalwart team to deliver, the task at hand becomes that much more difficult. Thankfully, the 165th was more than primed to address challenge. LTC Walters encapsulated the battalion's attitude to delivery: "My favorite acronym is VANI. It stands for 'Value Added, No Issues,' and that summed up the 165th."

A key player in the team at Abu Ghraib, assisting Major Edwards and Captain Qureishi, was a soldier commonly known as "The Mayor." Edwards explained: "What a great guy. One of the hardest working soldiers we had in the base. Our mayor was a Sergeant First Class infantryman." Walters added: "He was your stereotypical non-commissioned officer. Rough around the collar, straight shooter and had a work ethic like you can't imagine. He worked all hours of the day and night and was always totally selfless. For him, it was all about making life better for the soldiers in the unit. He brought our standard of living up to a remarkable level in Balad and when he had to start all over in Abu Ghraib, there was no doubt in anyone's mind who the forward operating base mayor was going to be and that was 'The Mayor.'"

Major Edwards added background color to the mayor: "When I got to Balad, Bob and the Command Sergeant Major were living in the back of the tactical operations center and there was a space for me and the operations officers. Our rooms were separated by plywood walls and

13. Locally Sourced

I hung a rain poncho liner over the front of the entrance of my door, which made it a poncho liner door!

"As it started to get really hot in the summer, I said to the mayor, 'It's so damn hot, I can't sleep. How can anyone sleep in this heat?' He went and got a fan off the Iraqi market and installed it in my little hooch and it blew right into my face. That fan was on 24/7. Later on we were able to get air conditioners into the tactical operations center and living areas. The problem with that is we had to drill holes into walls and that was like an open invitation to the population of mice in the area. Then we had to figure out a way to plug the holes."

Sourcing goods and items from the local economy was essential, but without local knowledge the task would have been nearly impossible. Edwards continued: "In Balad, we would have local Iraqi nationals come into the forward operating base and we would pay them to work with us. Guys would sweep, pick up trash, those sort of tasks. The idea at the time was to employ Iraqis that needed work and money. We didn't pay them a lot, but I can remember the mayor having a formation of Iraqis that were working for us, lining them up like an Army formation and paying them for the work they did that week. However, there were people who would try and play the system. You'd have guys show up on the Friday who hadn't been there the entire week and they'd want to get paid for the entire week. The mayor would snap at them and be like, 'You weren't here from Monday to Thursday. Get out of here,' which was quite funny to see sometimes.

"Another time, we were dealing with a lot of Iraqi contractors from a service perspective. People that would come onto the base at Abu Ghraib and bring in water, gravel or some sort of material and on a number of occasions we'd catch them trying to siphon fuel from our vehicles to put into their dump trucks or something similar. I remember once, the mayor caught one of the workers and said to me furiously, while this Iraqi guy was standing in front of us, 'We've got to ban this guy from our forward operating base. I caught him stealing gas from one of the trucks.' I would get one of the guys like Muhamed or Amar to translate to the guy what the mayor was saying while this Iraqi guy was standing there petrified. The mayor took that stuff super seriously."

The mayor's achievements went far beyond gas thieves and fan installation, as Edwards explained: "We were trying to transition from generator power to shore power in Balad, because we were living off hundreds of generators everywhere, which were running 24/7 and which frankly, after a while were going to break. The mayor had a requirement, to have two generators for the tactical operations center. One was for operation and one for backup, which was really smart. Something I would use later on in my career. It meant the center was never without power, because we were using two 10,000-watt generators. Bear in mind, a 10k generator would probably power an entire street.

"Then somehow, the mayor said, 'We're going to get shore power.' It took about half the battalion to pick up and carry this huge cable which was about two hundred meters long and drag it to wherever the mayor told us. We were in our physical training gear, had our shorts and t-shirts on as it was the middle of summer and in sweltering heat, trying to get this power connected, because that was going to make our life a lot easier. Abu Ghraib on the other hand lived off generators the whole time we were there. It never had the backbone of Balad, despite the mayor's best efforts."

Captain Romeo Qureishi dealt directly with the Iraqi employees and explained the key players in Abu Ghraib: "The same employees who helped to build up Balad, I took them with us to Abu Ghraib, which was great, because there were security issues with the people that were local. We paid them fairly, they were very happy and we treated them well.

"Amar was a younger guy, in his twenties and he focused on things that we needed in the office. It could be something as simple as a microwave, a phone, cleaning stuff, things like that. Muhamed was the construction guy. He got the laborers to clean up stuff, to build things, get wood, you name it. That's how I separated them logistically.

"Muhamed was in Abu Ghraib as a detainee for about ten years, under the Saddam Hussein rule. One of the first things I asked when he started working with us, was if he would be alright to work in Abu Ghraib, as it would be somewhat of a post traumatic experience. He said, 'No problem. I don't really know Abu Ghraib, only the inside of a cell here.' When he was a detainee, he never walked around, because whenever he walked out of his cell, they put a hood over his head.

"In terms of hands-on help, Muhamed was a big help with the two construction projects we had in Abu Ghraib. Building the tactical operations center into one of the main buildings and creating the living area. Where you'd see the paintings of Saddam Hussein in the photos, that was an old textile factory where the prisoners would make rugs and the giant looms were still present in the concrete. It was a desolate, damp and musty building that had ground water seeping from the ground. It was far from sanitary. They had looming machines in that area where the prisoners used to create stuff like carpets. That became offices. Muhamed helped us to source materials such as plywood, to help separate and create areas and also put desks in there. We even put in Astro-Turf, which sounds basic, but something like that in a place full of rocks and sand can help change your day. Those sorts of things really went a long way to help the soldiers."

Walters explained the budget available to the 165th in Abu Ghraib: "During combat operations, the United States Congress appropriates funding known as overseas contingency funding. This funding pot is flexible and allows deployed commanders to expend government

Battalion Commander's office at Abu Ghraib. Note the AstroTurf on the floor to make it a useable space (Romeo Qureishi's collection).

Temporary headquarters constructed in abandoned factory (Romeo Qureishi's collection).

funds as they deem appropriate with oversight provided by higher headquarters."

Edwards added: "I don't remember a budget but I had to leverage my network to arrange for engineering support. I was able to get a construction unit on the forward operating base to help with infrastructure. We worked the process as a request for a military order through the headquarters in Baghdad, tasking a unit to support. I did have a cash budget of $20K a month for improvement projects, but if necessary, we could request additional funds with justification. However, obtaining the physical funds was a trip to Baghdad or Balad where the contracting and finance hubs existed and that's a road you tried to avoid if possible."

Everybody loves a bargain. Given the moniker 'Captain Barterer,' by the Iraqi locals, Qureishi discussed his passion for ensuring the battalion's budget was used as frugally as possible: "I'm all about saving tax payers' money. The vendors, yes, they loved me because of the Middle Eastern roots of my surname, but they also loved me because I negotiated. The other logistics officers that I was friends with, the Iraqis would give them a price, say for example $500 for this pressure washer, the other guys would take it, thinking, 'We're at war, so you've got to take into account inflation.' I was like, 'No.' It was part of the culture. You were less of a man if you didn't barter! I bartered all the time.

"At the time we were trying to get Armor for our vehicles. The other guys said they couldn't get any. They normally gave 3mm, but I got 6mm, because I always doubled it. They wanted a thousand dollars per vehicle and I knew we were in war, but I said, 'How about five hundred bucks per vehicle? I have twenty vehicles I need done.' In the end I got it done for about six hundred per vehicle. Thank God we had it done, because we were surrounded by anarchy in Abu Ghraib.

"Our relationship with the Iraqis worked well. If we were honest with people, it doesn't matter if you don't speak the same language. At that point I'd already been to Bosnia and Kosovo and I learned in the military, it doesn't matter what country you go to, if you treat people humanely, they're going to do everything for you. Whether it be an Iraqi national that didn't know me from Adam or Amar."

Edwards added: "These were guys Romeo enlisted to help us run the battalion logistics, because they had easy access to places we didn't. They were Iraqi Muslims and could go to Baghdad, Tikrit, Mosul, almost anywhere in fact, untouched and unscathed. We kept these guys as employees in the battalion, providing us with creative solutions in a harsh environment."

Despite being highly praising of Qureishi's bartering skills, Edwards was no rookie in the marketplace. Edwards recalled: "Soon after arriving at Balad, I started to see the battalion through a different lens that they may have seen themselves through, because I hadn't actually been with them from the beginning. I was like fresh eyes and it's always good to get fresh eyes on anything, something I would always try and get on whichever forward operating bases I'd be on in the future, just to make sure I wasn't missing anything.

"When I got there, the staff functioned around me for all the logistical things that needed to happen in the battalion. We had a non-commissioned officer in the logistics shop who was a young sergeant. Great guy. He and I got in a Humvee and drove around Balad and there were units everywhere, most of which you had no idea what their function was. You'd be chatting with one unit and ask them, 'What do you do?' and they'd say, 'We break rocks. We're a construction unit.' The next one would be refining water, etc. I went round to each unit and got to grips with what they did. What I was learning as the executive officer, in this environment, you're going to have to barter a little bit or at least do a deal to exchange something for something, because the logistics had not caught up to where it was flowing yet.

"Parts for vehicles and other types of equipment were coming into logistical hubs and were going into bins labeled by a unit. So, think of these large bins in this open yard and it has your unit name on. If you are out in that yard, and I'm not saying this happened, people would say, I can't believe that unit got this or that. The only way at the beginning to get what you needed was to build relationships and build that confidence and trust with each other. If I had a 50 caliber barrel that the unit needed, but we needed sandbags, I'd gladly trade it, if it was the right trade. For example. The sergeant and I found a pallet of sandbags, which was a lot and we were able to work a deal with this unit to use those sandbags for the sleeping tents and lining the floors of the Humvees. They wouldn't do anything against an IED, but it gave us a little bit of security and self confidence that I had something between me and the ground. We were all issued a flak vest, but I brought two or three with me because of all the different units I'd been in and I would sit on one and wrap it around my waist. Some people would hang them on the doors. The vests did absolutely nothing, but it made you feel good! Anyway, I exchanged something for the sandbags and got what I needed for the 165th. Once, I also arranged for 50 caliber barrels for the long-range surveillance company, because they were burning through them rapidly. They needed five and we were able to make that happen in Balad where I had a good connection in the brigade support battalion. It happened to be the same brigade that I served in years before as an intelligence officer and company commander.

"Another time, the long-range surveillance commander came to me and said, 'We need handheld thermals.' I ended up spending about two days looking for handheld thermals, which was basically a camera with thermal capability that they could use on the hide site. I don't know how I paid for them, but I sorted something out with another unit. Every time I did something for the long-range surveillance company I always felt I was getting credits, because these were always going to be the guys that would take me somewhere."

During Major Edwards' onsite travels in Balad, he would sometimes encounter some rather interesting items: "One of the guys in the brigade support battalion had a conex full of weapons that they'd confiscated over the previous six months. This guy said, 'You want to see the weapons we've confiscated?' I'm like, 'Yeah. That would be great.'

"He opens up the conex and it was full of armaments, including gold and silver plated AK-47's, which was crazy. The one thing I'll never forget was a pistol grip machine gun, looked like a .30 caliber, probably from Korea in World War II, still in the crate. They opened up the crate and it was in this perfect packaging, with the grease still on it when it left the factory."

Honesty, as Captain Qureishi mentioned, is a strong foundation of any relationship and it soon became apparent that Amar and Muhamed were men of integrity. Edwards explained: "On one occasion, Romeo and I had told Amar we needed a tarp made for our maintenance guys so that they could work on the vehicles in the shade.

"Amar went to Baghdad and got a tarp. He told Romeo, 'It's going to be $2,500.' We said, 'That's fine. Sounds good.' Romeo probably talked him down! Amar went and got the tarp made and when he came back he said, 'I need to get paid.' We gave him some paperwork to take to the finance office in Balad, then he came back to Abu Ghraib.

"About two or three days later he came directly to me and said, 'I have a problem.' I said, 'What's the problem Amar? Didn't you get paid?' He replies, 'Yes, I got paid, but they paid me $25,000.' They'd added a zero by accident. Amar was an Iraqi citizen and could have taken that money, gone back home and never come back to Abu Ghraib. Instead he told me, 'I've been overpaid, what should I do?' I said, 'Let's take out the money that's owed to you and we'll take the rest of it and secure it in the little battalion safe.' The point is, he was an honest guy and wanted to make a living, but he wasn't a thief. On a number of occasions, he told me, 'I just want to save enough money to buy my mother a refrigerator,' and eventually he achieved his goal from the money he earned working for us, which he was very proud of. He also ended up buying himself a red BMW 325 down in Umm Qasr, which was the only medium depth port that services Iraq, directly next to Camp Bucca on the Iraq/Kuwait border. He was so proud of that car and once he bought it, he drove up to Abu Ghraib and drove us around the compound.

"Back to the overpayment. Once Amar gave us the balance of the money, we stored it in the safe and I called the finance office in Balad. 'You've overpaid one of our contractors and I need you guys to come and pick up your money.' The finance officer said, 'Sure. Where's it at and when do you want us to come and get it?' I replied, 'You can come and get it tomorrow if you like, or any day which works for you. By the way, we're at Abu Ghraib.' The moment I mentioned where we were, he was like, 'Er, Sir, that's in Anbar and that's really dangerous. I'm not coming down there.' I said, 'No, no. You need to come down here and pick up your money. We don't have the manpower to put people on the road to go back to Balad and return it.'

"About two days later, this young finance officer shows up at Abu Ghraib and we give him the money and he says to me, 'Is there any way I can fly back to Balad?' I said, 'The only aircraft coming in here are usually Black Hawks that are bringing detainees in. These are battlefield combat vehicles. I'm not in the business of arranging flights back to Balad, so you probably need to get a ride from a ground convoy.' He didn't look very happy."

"Just wanted to say a few words about Muhamed and Amar. I'm not sure where Amar is, but wherever he is, I hope he's safe. Unfortunately, we lost Muhamed about three weeks after we left Iraq in February 2004. We got word that he'd been killed at a checkpoint. RIP old friend."

14

Beef Jerky

"The power of getting to know one another is so immense, eclipsed only by first getting to know ourselves."—Bryant McGill

A sturdy infrastructure was paramount to the success of the 165th's mission in Abu Gharib; however, at the tactical level, simple routines provided the informal backbone to maintaining good staff morale and unit cohesion. Major Edwards explained: "Your stress levels, regardless of what people say, are ultra-high in this kind of environment, so we were always looking for ways to make the quality of our days better, or funnier, to ease the tension. When we were in Balad, we would have Sunday haircuts and one of the things I was normally responsible for was to find some good coffee beans somewhere on the base while we had our hair cut. I would go around to the infantry brigade and our higher headquarters and I'd negotiate with some people to try and get a bag of coffee that they'd had sent to them. In the early days you had to make do with what was on base, because our mail cycle was over three or four weeks at a time, which was a pretty long time between deliveries from the home front, so trading was quite common amongst soldiers. When it came to coffee, I raised my game to make sure I returned with the goods.

"Coffee and haircuts were an example of a routine that unofficially facilitated bonding in the unit. I can remember more than once our operations sergeant major cutting my hair and I don't think he actually knew how to cut hair. In fact, I know he didn't. But we didn't care. It was more that you could sit down, have a cup of coffee and catch up."

"Also, a lot of times when we were working and tired, we had some downtime and would do things like watch DVD's. Someone had mailed a boxset of the *Sopranos* series and we would take the disks and pass them around. These were little things we did to keep ourselves motivated and happy, but also watching a U.S. television show would give you a taste of home. If you had an hour in the evening and wanted a little downtime for yourself, you'd maybe go to where you slept and relaxed, and you could watch an episode of that or sometimes the other soldiers would watch an episode together. We would always say, 'Only watch one episode at a time,' in that way you had something to look forward to and it also became a routine. Once in a while though, you'd want to binge watch and stay up all night and watch a bundle of episodes."

When the chance came to add a touch of style to the culinary offerings at the tactical operations center, Edwards seized the opportunity: "Bob had asked me to go down to Ramadi as we had a couple of long-range surveillance guys that were stationed down there who were working with the 3rd Armored Cavalry Regiment. Both of Saddam Hussein's sons had palaces down there and one day I was with one of the soldiers from our battalion and we went to see the palace. This place had been hit with a joint direct attack munition. The inside was destroyed and the walls crumbling and when I walked into the entrance and looked up, I could see straight through the palace ceiling at this cylindrical hole. The walls were made of marble and you could go in and go up on the balcony areas and see over the river. It was a pretty interesting place.

"Back in Balad at the time, we had these packages of sausages and cheese that we'd been sent and we would cut them up so we could share them out. The problem was, we didn't have a proper chopping board, so on this day, we took a sledgehammer and took a piece of marble off the wall. I brought it back to Balad and in addition to our coffee pot, we now had a marble chopping board, which we cleaned up real nice."

From a commander's perspective routines were essential to success on a daily basis. LTC Walters shared his view: "Every day there were things you had to do. Update briefings were part of our 'battle rhythm,' which was like our daily schedule. In those briefings, the staff would inform myself and the other leaders in the battalion what was happening within their particular lane. For example, Romeo would give a logistics update, etc.

"Then there was battlefield circulation. You had junior leaders checking up on your soldiers and the more senior leaders carrying out spot checks. That's where commanders and leaders went out to check certain things around the areas that the soldiers were responsible for. Going through those perimeter security towers, checking they knew what their instructions were, making sure their weapons were prepared to be employed if necessary and making sure the soldiers hadn't been stuck up there by themselves for too many hours. That was battlefield circulation. Then we would respond to incidents that occurred. Visitors would often come in from Baghdad and we would give them an update brief on what was happening at the forward operating base.

"Then you also got calls from the higher headquarters, with tasks. Sometimes it was an operational task, other times it was logistical. If it was a logistics task, I would give it to Bill and he would work with Romeo to come up with a plan to execute it. If it was an operations task, then the operations officer would come up with a way to do it, with one of the companies to execute that operation. Whatever task or duty you were undertaking, the routine was essential to keep your daily focus."

Keeping focus is essential in a combat zone environment, but sometimes the local surroundings made that task more difficult. Edwards explained: "In the northwest of Abu Ghraib prison, there was a really tall apartment building that was outside of the forward operating base, but had direct access into the logistics support area, where we lived. I was always concerned about that apartment building, because it was part of the little town or village that was next to the prison. Also, in that same corner, opposite one of our towers, was a mosque that was 24/7 with a massive loudspeaker that was really annoying. The only thing that separated the tower from the mosque was a road.

"Here's a little story about that road. Soon after we were getting settled in early December, doing checks to make sure everyone was on task, something strange, but almost comical happened. I was standing up there in the tower on battlefield circulation and on this particular night a Bradley Fighting vehicle from some other unit came rolling down this road, firing their 25mm chain gun and I didn't even know what they were shooting at. Also, they were by themselves, which was really odd, because normally there were two vehicles together. Then, while they were firing this weapon, they locked the brakes and skidded across the road and started motoring in the other direction. We were just standing there looking, wondering what the heck was going on! It was probably a unit responsible for that land or perhaps someone went past his unit's boundary.

"Anyway, back to the speaker. On this occasion, I was up there and checking on two soldiers up in the north tower while the speaker was blasting away with prayers in Arabic. It was a funny conversation because as I'm standing there talking to the two guys in the tower and this speaker is going at prayer time, I can barely hear myself, never mind what the soldiers are saying. We were shouting to each other. One of them asked, 'Sir. Is there any way we can just shoot that speaker? We won't hurt anyone, we're just going to shoot the speaker.' I replied, 'I'm afraid not. It's just something we can't do. Put some earplugs in.' However, I totally understood where they were coming from and while standing there, empathized with their reasoning behind the question. We could even hear it from the center of the base from our cots in a hardstand building. It was really that loud."

Walters added: "I think the prayers happened five times a day if memory serves me correct. Dawn, dusk and three other times. That doesn't mean that someone was up all the time because most of it was probably pre-recorded. It was very close and very loud because it was designed to reach out to the whole village of Abu Ghraib. All the inhabitants knew it was time for prayer and we just happened to be right next to it and the tower was elevated to a similar height of the speaker at the mosque on the wall. It was definitely unpleasant when that thing started blaring out for the young soldiers that were up there, but there was nothing we could do.

"Unless there was somebody next to the speaker shooting at us, there's no way we could have shot in that direction. Calling to pray was not aggressive and not something we needed to respond with lethal force. Bill gave those young soldiers the absolutely correct guidance at that point. If we'd have shot the speaker, we would have had an issue with the village inhabitants and the imam who ran the mosque. We would have got a temporary reprieve from the noise, but there would have been a cost associated with it."

Edwards continued: "In terms of day-to-day routine, it was exactly as Bob described. We were all working all the time, because you're trying to keep all the pieces together. For me, having responsibility of the staff and making sure everyone was on task and doing the things they needed to do and coordinating with the company commanders in the battalion, was a full-time job. That in itself also established routine for the soldiers, because they knew they had work to do.

"We would also, occasionally work in hip-pocket training (also known as opportunity training, or 'just in time' training, due to its ad lib nature). We would keep ourselves at the highest level of training we could do, including shooting our weapons all the time in a training environment, so that we could stay proficient and keep our skills sharp.

14. Beef Jerky

"I'd been trained as an officer under some great leaders and one thing I'd learned is that you want to have those individual conversations with soldiers, to understand what people were going through and understand how their families are doing. Bob reinforced this. Then when I was a battalion commander years later, I was establishing those type of routines for my unit. Lieutenants and captains would come up to me and say, 'That was really great that you did that. It kept us looking forward.' The deployments are often long, especially for regular Army units. They were anywhere between twelve and fourteen months and sometimes units would get tied over for fifteen months. So, from a military perspective, there was something to do in order to keep yourself engaged and working towards the mission."

Walters added: "From my perspective the soldiers you're serving with, communication happens in a few different ways. The more senior members of the staff like Bill, the operations officer, the command sergeant major; we would sometimes eat at the same time together and during the conversation while we were eating someone would say, 'What's going on with your family back home?' That happened frequently. Most of my conversations were with the senior folks, but I didn't necessarily have those conversations with the junior staff, unless it was during battlefield circulation."

Armed with a special culinary prop, Walters recalled his method of engaging with the junior soldiers: "I'd received a box from a church group back home that had a bunch of beef jerky in it. On battlefield circulation, I would carry little baggies of that around and at 2am, if I was checking that tower, I'd offer the soldier some beef jerky. This was after I'd checked their weapons were working, they had water, how long they had been up on duty and that sort of stuff. At that point I'd ask where he or she was from in the States and get into a little bit of a conversation with them. The beef jerky was like an icebreaker and after offering it, they'd usually say, 'Sure,' and then we'd start chatting a little bit. You'd learn about the family and the soldiers during time like that. It might be weeks before I bump into that soldier again, so it certainly wasn't a routine encounter, but for many, including myself, it was time well spent.

"It's important to know though, as a senior officer you shouldn't pry, especially into some young soldier's life, because not everyone had a positive homelife. Unless the young troop wanted to share or brought up the topic, then that was fine, but otherwise, you needed to be conscious that there were certain lines you didn't want to cross. They had

115

their privacy and private family lives and if that soldier didn't want to peel back the layers of that onion and share it with anyone, you needed to be respectful of that."

Major Edwards added: "Everything is situationally dependent. A lot of the times conversations were done over meals or a cup of coffee. You had to be able to navigate the situation you were in and the technique you used with that jerky or equivalent was often very important on a number of levels."

15

Feeding Time at Abu Ghraib

"An army marches on its stomach."—Napoleon

Fueling a battalion correctly is an essential fundamental need of any military engine. Major Edwards explained the catering provision at Abu Ghraib: "When we arrived, there wasn't an established dining facility. There was a contracted British company employing a couple of Iraqi nationals to prepare food and as Romeo said, 'It seemed that for the first month, all we ate was chicken nuggets and French fries.' We served ourselves out of what we called our mobile kitchen, which was basically an 'ad hoc' mess hall and we just sat down wherever we found a spot. That's when we put into motion setting up the dining facility and getting the contract in place.

"We started to make logistics runs into Baghdad or Baghdad International Airport to pick up what we called Class 1 food, so we could cook for ourselves until the standard of the contract dining facility got to a point where Bob was comfortable with the offering. Apart from that we found ourselves eating a lot of MREs, straight out of the box."

Assistant Operations Officer Mike Flentie added: "The first year of the war, the logistics struggled to keep up with the needs. We were on MREs, breakfast, lunch and dinner. We had *country captain chicken* for about sixty days when we were in Balad. That was the only thing the supply chain had for dinner. In theory, there was a variety, but when you eat them for several months, they all taste the same. I know everyone in the battalion lost massive amounts of weight. I was 132 lbs when I went to Iraq and I was 110 lbs when I came home from Abu Ghraib. My wife hardly recognized me.

"Me and the ops sergeant major used to joke. He was a little on the

Mike Flentie making things happen on the satellite phone (Mike Flentie's collection).

chunky side when he arrived and he had one of those military belts and put a little black mark on it to show how much he'd lost. By the time we'd left, he had a huge tail hanging down from his belt, with about ten check marks on it where he'd lost weight.

"The only thing I could stomach to eat was this wheat snack bread which came in the MRE. It was horrid and I was the only one who ate it. I'd eat it with peanut butter for breakfast every morning. LTC Walters and Major Edwards never ate it. The way we were set up in the tactical operations center, I was facing a wall with my computer, and they were based in the center looking at the back of me. They would flick the wheat snack bread to me every day, which would hit me at the back of my head. I'd be piling it up on my desk for breakfast and sometimes lunch. They started to call me 'Flentie Bread!'"

Despite an unorthodox and rocky start, feeding at Abu Ghraib for the 165th was executed with military precision. Edwards explained: "There were scheduled mealtimes for breakfast, lunch and dinner. If you were on duty, your fellow soldiers would take care of you. If you were in the tower for example, we'd take care of one another, because there was never a time that you weren't on duty. Sometimes it was eat when you could, but other times, you'd follow the schedule. Either way, nobody starved.

"If you didn't have the chance to make one of the feeding slots, we ensured that soldiers had access to food. We had packages of food being sent to us from friends and family by this stage. At the beginning it would take about three to four weeks for them to come through, but as time went on we became more proficient with our systems. However, if you missed a chow time, there was always an MRE available, which contained about 3,500 calories and you could pick whatever you wanted out of it. In Mike Flentie's case, that was usually the bread!"

At times like these, it's natural to yearn for home comforts. Walters' fantasy meal of choice: "Whenever I found myself in an austere environment, what I would crave was a Burger King double beef Whopper with cheese, minus ketchup, plus mustard." Edwards added: "I used to ask my dad to vacuum seal cinnamon sugar bagels. He'd vacuum sealed a bunch of them and even though they'd arrive three weeks later, they'd still be fresh. That would be a great treat when they arrived."

Edwards continued: "About six weeks after we arrived, we started working with some new contractors and construction guys, creating a dining area. We set up our mobile kitchen trailer in the northwest corner of the forward operating base and started cooking our meals. We painted the walls white, had plastic stand up tables with tablecloths, bench seats, individual chairs and clean floors.

"The food service was done cafeteria style. We had people cooking the food and serving the meals, which got better over time, but compared to the chicken nugget scenario, it was luxury. Later on, we even got ice cream, which was important because I know Bob likes it! I have to say though, contrary to many, I was always a fan of Army chow. I genuinely liked Army food. Our food service personnel did the best they could with what they had. I was a headquarter service company commander before I came to 165th years before and I ran a mess section and we were always trying to be creative with the food. Here's an example from Labor Day 2003.

"We were trying to do something nice for the unit because it was a national holiday, so I said to Bob, 'Maybe I can hop on an RC-12 and buy some stuff to barbeque? Some chicken, pork chops etc.' I went to the aviation unit and jumped in this RC-12, which is a little military utility aircraft and we headed to Kuwait.

"We had a rear detachment in Germany, but we also had a couple of people in Kuwait at Camp Doha that would help us with other logistics things we might need. I flew down there with just me and two pilots in the plane. One of them asked me, 'What are you doing?' and I replied, 'I'm going to buy some meat for a barbeque for Labor Day.' He says, 'Just make sure you don't go over our weight limit or we aren't going to be able to take off!'

"I had a couple of coolers full of dry ice and I filled them up. When I got back, I gave the meat to the mess section and we had a pretty nice barbeque for Labor Day. Most importantly, we gave the soldiers a little taste of home.

"As the dining came together at Abu Ghraib, we started to get drinks coming in like shelf milk, which had a long life and didn't need to stay cold. We also had juice boxes. We couldn't afford to drink local population water in case of the potential casualties that could occur if it was not clean, so we stuck with bottled water. Also, there was always tea and coffee available. My most memorable meal was breakfast, because they did a pretty good job of getting together eggs, grits and things like that."

Assistant Operations Officer Mike Flentie recalled: "I love coffee. We had a good stockpile of it which our spouses would send over from Europe. We had one of those old percolator coffee pots, but LTC Walters' coffee requirement for strength was literally like tar. It was undrinkable. So I switched over to tea. Americans don't drink that much tea and the U.S. soldiers in Abu Ghraib certainly didn't drink tea, so I would get shit every day! 'Ohhh. Here's the tea drinker.'"

Whether it be tea, coffee or water, hydration was an essential part of every soldier's daily routine. Walters explained: "We had command emphasis on personal hygiene and sanitation, but hydration was probably number one on that list. We drank a lot of coffee to be alert, but we were constantly emphasizing the need to drink plenty of water.

"By the time we got to Abu Ghraib, the logistics had not caught up with the operational force. In terms of the water, we had to take it out of the Euphrates or Tigris rivers and then we'd run it through the reverse osmosis purification unit in order to make it potable for the soldiers. As the infrastructure improved, the environment became more developed and we started getting bottled water. Unfortunately, we never saw a purification unit in Abu Ghraib, but with this emphasis on hydration, you'd still see people carrying a rifle in one hand and a bottle of water in the other. This is exactly what we wanted to see. If we saw a soldier without a bottle in their hand or wearing a camel back water container, the leaders would ask, 'Where's your water?' because we wanted to emphasize that.

"The amount of water we wanted the soldiers to drink varied in relation to the weather. We would have a wet bulb globe test to accurately give us an indication of what kind of weather we were in. That would let us know how hot it was and the humidity in the air, so you got the 'feels like' temperature. The air temperature might be 100 degrees, but add in the humidity and it would often feel like 115."

Although hydration was essential, certain beverages were prohibited. Edwards explained: "There's a photo of me and Mike Flentie in the tactical operation center in Balad holding a beer, let me point out there was no alcohol in it. As the theater matured, the Army brought in non-alcoholic beer. The food service there was really getting good by that time and the logistics guys were bringing in the 'near beer' which would be a knock-off version of a well-known brand. That picture of Mike and I, we were drinking the near beer and dreaming of real beer.

"One of the things that happened towards the end of our time in

Captain Mike Flentie (left) and Major Edwards enjoying a "non-alcoholic" moment (William Edwards' collection).

Abu Ghraib was that they started giving us energy drinks, like Monster and Red Bull. The issue with those drinks is that they would boost your energy with caffeine which is actually a diuretic in so much as they don't hydrate your body. Similar to coffee. If you drink a lot of that, you'll soon get dehydrated."

Despite alcohol being prohibited, the capacity for it slipping through the net always existed. Captain Romeo Qureishi recalled: "A lot of the other personnel who'd been to Abu Ghraib before said, 'Hey, Romeo. There's three things you've got to watch out for. Alcohol, drugs and prostitution.' I'm like, 'What?' How's that possible. This was a military operation. These were all violations of General Order Number One."

Walters explained: "General Order Number One was issued by the U.S. Central Command, located at MacDill Air Force base, Florida. They also had a command post in Kuwait. That four-star geographic combatant commander issued General Order Number One, which essentially says, 'You're not allowed to drink alcohol, possess pornographic material, have sexual activity' and several other things to help soldiers maintain order and discipline. It's changed a bit since 2003, but the bulk is the same. It was applicable to all military personnel who had deployed in a U.S. Central Command, which meant Kuwait, Iraq, Afghanistan, etc. We were clearly under that order, so every single member was briefed prior to deploying.

"Did soldiers try to do things under the radar of their leadership while deployed? Yes. The bulk of the personnel were between seventeen to twenty-four years old and the leadership was typically a little bit older than that. The leadership tended to be more mature with their decisions, but some of the junior soldiers would try to take advantage when the opportunity presented itself. There was always a way for someone to get alcohol and consume it, but when soldiers were walking around with loaded weapons, there was a chance a poor decision or a negligent discharge could result in the injury or death of a fellow soldier.

"When Romeo got wind that there were some violations of General Order Number One in Abu Ghraib, that was indicative that the chain of command in place at the time was not effectively leading their soldiers and taking corrective action.

"The leaders would also need to do health and welfare inspections, where they would show up unexpectedly and look for contraband items among the soldiers' personal items. There were different ways their loved ones could send these items over and conceal them. For example, they could take a bottle of mouthwash, dump it out and put vodka inside and then send it. If it got through the screening that the military postal service provided, the soldiers could get their hands on some alcohol. The other way a soldier could do it was to approach the contractors who then had access to the local economy. Even though it's a Muslim country, there's still alcohol there. If they gave money, they could ask them to bring something back in. However, it was usually pretty easy to spot. For example, I'd see Bill fourteen hours a day, so I'd know immediately if he was intoxicated, then it would be my responsibility to do health and welfare for the whole area."

A couple of months down the line, after the discovery of a highly confidential disk, soldiers would be ordered to destroy their own personal collections of revealing material, literally bringing tears to their eyes. For now, the focus was on staying alive in Abu Ghraib.

16

Christmas Day

"Victory was for those willing to fight and die. Intellectuals could theorize until they sucked their thumbs right off their hands, but in the real world, power still flowed from the barrel of a gun."
—Mark Bowden, *Black Hawk Down:*
A Story of Modern War

While the 165th were settling into their surroundings, for many others around the world, December signified the build up to Christmas. In fact, just down the road in Camp Victory, Baghdad, the WWE wrestling stars put on a festive performance for the coalition troops, which included the likes of John Cena and Steve Austin. Major Edwards commented: "I had no knowledge of this going on. What's interesting about that is that even though we were only about ten miles apart, the environments were totally different. It was almost like two separate worlds in parallel. There's this show going on in Camp Victory and we were living in disgust at Abu Ghraib."

LTC Walters added: "When we did admin logistics convoy, or pushed a surveillance team out, we did it out of necessity. Something like this was not mission related, it was one of those 'Nice to do' things. Putting together a convoy to go from Abu Ghraib over to Victory to get the soldiers to attend a concert, is something we wouldn't have done, even if we had been aware. The risk versus the gain would have told us that putting a hundred soldiers' lives at risk to go over and watch the wrestlers was not an option."

Instead, the 165th Battalion had its own version of festive events to keep them occupied at Abu Ghraib. Walters recalled an incident in mid–December: "We were in the tactical operations center and all of a sudden I heard gunfire coming from one of the towers. We went up and there was a young soldier who was a little bit rattled. Across the field there was a road and on that road was a vehicle on fire with a crowd of Iraqi locals around it.

"By this time, other members of the leadership had also made their way up to the tower. I asked what happened and the soldier said the vehicle was coming down the road and there was a guy hanging out of it with a gun and he engaged. I said, 'Okay.' I asked what happened next and he said, 'The vehicle went out of control, sat there for a few minutes and caught fire.'

"Within the rules of engagement, you don't have to wait for the guy with the gun to shoot at you in order to shoot. When they point a gun at you, that's sufficient. What happened later, a civil affairs officer, which is another branch within the Army, which does a lot of interface with the locals, came and asked me about the event, which I duly described. He said, 'What are you doing with that soldier?' and I said, 'What do you mean?' 'He killed a sheik's son. He needs to be prosecuted.' This guy was senior to me. I said, 'It was nighttime and he didn't know the guy was a sheik's son. He had a gun pointing at him and responded according to the rules of engagement. There's cars driving down that road all day and night long and we don't shoot at any of them unless they present a threat to the soldiers that are here guarding the detainees at the base.' He said, 'They didn't find a weapon in the vehicle.' I said, 'I saw at least twenty Iraqi civilians around that vehicle and if there had been a weapon in it, they would have taken it. They wouldn't have just left it in there for investigators the next day to find the weapon.' He was up in arms about that.

"There was an investigation and when the investigators came, I told them what happened and they were happy with that. No further action was taken."

While Camp Victory had John Cena and Steve Austin, Abu Ghraib had their ops sergeant major. Walters explained the events of Christmas Eve 2003: "Around this time of year we would receive packages from our families. Inside would be cookies, candy, the kind of stuff that you would expect to be shipped to soldiers that have been deployed during holidays. On the evening of December 24, 2003, the ops sergeant major had been going around dressed in this Santa suit that somebody had sent him, handing out goodies and spreading the joy of Christmas.

"Suddenly, we came under heavy incoming mortar fire. When these types of things happen, there's a number of military tasks that need to be addressed immediately. You have to call in troops in contact to headquarters, assess any damage incurred from the attack and reinforce your security posture in case there's a follow on at the entry control point or somewhere else along the perimeter. And if soldiers are badly wounded you had to do a 'Nine Line,' which is a MEDEVAC call to request helicopter evacuation of a soldier who had been injured.

"Whenever an attack occurred, everybody knew what their job was and got into that mindset—and it didn't matter if you were in your duty uniform or in a Santa suit. Mike Flentie and the battalion signal officer were in another hard stand building near to the tactical operation center which was about twenty meters away. As Mike and the signal officer were standing in the doorway of this building overlooking this area, the ops sergeant major ran across under mortar fire, while they were shouting, 'Come on, come on.'

"From my perspective, at the time of the attack, I distinctly remember being with some soldiers who were working the radios, and I saw someone running through the tactical operation center in his Santa suit. He was carrying his M16 rifle in one hand, a radio in the other and a big Churchill cigar in his mouth. It was quite the scene."

Meanwhile, back in Germany, Walters' wife, Nancy, gave her version of events from the end of a phone on Christmas Eve 2003: "My daughter Daytona called and said she was coming back for this Christmas because she wanted to be there to speak with Bob on the phone or in case he came home. We did Christmas with Daytona and a close friend of ours, but decided to do Christmas differently, which was common for many spouses when military soldiers were deployed. We didn't decorate the tree the same way, I didn't cook food, we ordered out for Chinese food and we drank eggnog and watched movies all day. Then the phone rang.

"I received a call from Bob, which was the best Christmas present I could have ever received, but during the call I heard the word screamed in the background 'INCOMING.' There was an explosion and the phone went dead. In the other room was Daytona and a soldier's wife, a close battle buddy of mine, that was alone and spending the day with us. I could barely feel my legs and by the grace of God I was calm enough to immediately call our rear detachment, let them know what happened and to please call me as soon as they had info. As a commander's spouse one of my personal philosophies is that I do not say anything unless there is something to tell. I left Daytona and the other wife in the room laughing and enjoying themselves, because her husband was with Bob.

Since I had nothing to tell them I wasn't about to tell them what had just gone down.

"Somehow, I got up and went back into the living room, had another eggnog, put on an Oscar winning performance and acted like everything was all right. However, in my mind, I was already trying to work out my game plan on being told bad news, with Daytona sitting by me, how I'd tell Martina back in the States, how I was going to tell Bob's mother, and who else who would be impacted if there was a knock at the door. So many things go through your mind. I was thinking, they won't notify you on the phone, they'll knock on the door. I told Daytona that her father said he loved her and he was putting together an email to Martina to let her know he loved her also.

"It took four hours before I got the update. It turned out to be a Christmas miracle, because no one was hurt that day in our unit."

By August 2003, detainee numbers at Abu Ghraib were estimated at less than a thousand. By September that had shot up to over six thousand and rising, with about three hundred military police officers to guard them. Walters added: "The impact on us with an increase in detainee population came in two ways. Security and base operations, and the infrastructure. In terms of security, the more detainees that came in, we had to have our entry control point procedures well rehearsed and executed. When the vehicles came to the entry control point at Abu Ghraib, they had to be searched to make sure there were no explosives or hostile armed personnel on board. These checks were conducted behind blast walls, so in case there was a vehicle with an IED on board and it went off, the most we would lose would be that first guard at the security entry control point and not half the camp. In terms of security around the detainees, that was up to the military police and did not impact the 165th Battalion.

"As far as base operations go, with an increase in detainees came the need for infrastructure improvement, which in turn meant increasing logistical vehicles coming into the compound. That included sewage removal, water, food and additional tents for those in the fenced compound. Meantime, Bill and the team were still doing infrastructure improvement with our mayor, under contract, repairing the wall, getting the sniper blind up so the apartment building next to the prison didn't have a sniper taking shots at us."

Inside Abu Ghraib

Edwards added: "As the population grew, our footprint to me felt smaller. It seemed like we were surrounded, which we were. We were in the center of all these different detainees holding areas. We were like a little small island in among everyone and as the number of detainees increased, our requirement to react also did."

Attacks on Abu Ghraib came in all shapes and sizes, and the main offenders were not strangers to the U.S. Army. Walters explained: "The ones we were concerned about mainly were the Sunni tribes that were in the Anbar region, which included Fallujah, Ramadi and all points west of Baghdad, which is where we were located. There was a large population of them in the area. The Sunnis were particularly upset with the Americans because they had been in control of Iraq and many of them were in leadership positions within the Iraqi Army prior to us coming in and overthrowing Saddam Hussein.

"The Shias didn't particularly like us either, but there wasn't as much of a concentration of them. They were further south in Karbala and Nijaf and in Baghdad of course. We didn't have any problems with the Kurds who were up in the north and eastern points of the country. It was mainly Sunni tribes in that area."

Edwards added: "AQI (Al Qaeda Iraq) hadn't actually formed yet and we were still dealing with the TWJ (Tawhid w'al Jihad) remnants, which was the predecessor to AQI. If you look at a timeline of how this all developed, you had TWJ, AQI, probably some splinters off of that and then now what's become ISIS. We were in the middle of Anbar in the Sunni Triangle, where there was a lot of disconnect and uprising, in terms of how the tables had turned after the invasion and the power shifts that were taking place. We were right in the middle of political crossfire."

Roll the clock back two weeks and human intelligence had reported a high likelihood of an attack at Abu Ghraib on Christmas Day. At the time, there were rumors that Jordanian jihadist and key insurgency leader Abu Musab al-Zarqawi was getting people arrested on purpose so they could be spies inside the prison. Walters explained: "That's exactly the type of stuff we would be looking for, to determine if they were planning any attacks and whether they were coordinating them with the detainees on the inside. We were getting regular intelligence reports of that occurring and that's why we needed to do something on this occasion to display our capability and serve as a deterrent."

Based on the information from the human intelligence company,

16. Christmas Day

Walters threw some light on the intended counter strike plan from the 165th: "It was a Christian holiday and one which was celebrated heavily in the U.S. By attacking the prison on that day, the insurgents were hoping to make a significant statement. I decided to go to the brigade commander and said, 'Human intelligence suggests we may be under attack at Abu Ghraib on the 25th of December. I'd like to do a show of force.' He replied, 'What do you mean?' I said, 'I've got a buddy that's a helicopter aviation battalion commander in Balad and he can come down here with a couple of aircrafts. We can have those come in and we can bring in a couple of teams of long-range surveillance soldiers and they can immediately reinforce the wall.' By conducting a show of force, the intention was to surprise anybody who was watching the facility, including the detainees inside, the locals outside and any insurgents that were planning an attack. The brigade commander approved the plan of action.

"We linked with the guys in Balad and did some rehearsals up there. Additionally, we briefed the other tenant units prior to the event and the military police were on board, participating on the ground. On Christmas Day at midday, we executed that mission."

"We flew in from Balad on two Black Hawk helicopters. My buddy was the battalion commander of this particular aviation element, and he was the pilot in command of one of the aircrafts, while I was flying in the other. He was a former night stalker from Taskforce 160th Special Operations Aviation Regiment.

"Inside the Black Hawk all the passenger seats were removed, and it was just an open area with everybody huddled on their hands and knees. In the aircraft I was in, there was the pilot and then one crew chief hanging out with a machine gun on one side and on the other were the second pilot and crew chief. When the craft landed, crew chiefs would assist the maintenance crew to ensure that the helicopter was flight worthy.

"It's worth noting that helicopters were routine travel, in and around our combat zone. They used them for logistics purposes, so helicopters coming in and landing was not unusual at all. We had a designated helicopter landing zone, and the pilots all had the coordinates so they could plug it into their GPS. We would not receive a notification if a helicopter was coming in, unless it was bringing in something directly for us logistically, then our headquarters would be notified, telling us at the agreed time we would be receiving goods, mail, or whatever it was. We would then have a detail to meet the helicopters and download whatever was coming in. If they were bringing in or moving detainees, we would not be notified, because we weren't involved with detainee handling. The military police would be notified as would the interrogation center of detainees moving in and out of Abu Ghraib, by helicopter or vehicle. On this day, the presence of the helicopters arrived in a manner that let everyone know that this was not a routine visit.

"Our designated fast rope site was over a dirt road in the center of the prison. A fast rope site is where a helicopter comes in, reaches its spot, stops and hovers over the site. The plan was for those two helicopters to approach both sides of the fenced-in portion of the detention area that was inside the forward operating base, making a firm show of force.

"Mike Flentie was in the guard tower and to Mike's amusement, when the Black Hawk I was in reached its fast rope site, it caused a bit of chaos with the detainees in the main yard. The Iraqi prisoners during the day would hang their blankets up on the wires around the tented areas, to air them out. When the Black Hawk arrived, it sent the blankets all over the place as this sea of detainees all watched this demonstration come in.

Christmas Day—one of the Black Hawks on a fast rope approach to demonstrate a show of force (William Edwards' collection).

16. Christmas Day

"Once the Black Hawk established its hover at the site, the pilot gave the command, 'Ropes out,' at which point the first roper, who happened to be me, kicked the ropes out, which had been coiled up on the floor inside the aircraft. I slid down and when I hit the ground, I ran off to the closest guard tower. The second roper did the same and it only took a minute or two for all of the ropers to safely fast rope down and reach the guard towers.

"After all the ropers were out, the crew chief reached over and pulled a metal safety pin, which released the rope to fall to the ground. The guys on the ground were then in charge of collecting the ropes. Once on the ground, we all reinforced the towers around the detainees for the show of force.

"In December the temperature was around 75 Fahrenheit on average and then it would get much cooler at night. All the guys who were doing the fast-roping had what we called our snivel gear on, which was basically layering up with hats, scarves, long underwear etc."

"Back to the show of force. When the aircraft came in, the soldiers slid down the ropes on the fast rope site and we reinforced the towers,

Hovering over the fast rope site. LTC Walters can be seen running, rifle in hand, bottom left (William Edwards' collection).

131

Top: Soldiers running to the towers to enforce the show of force. *Bottom:* All ropers away, cut rope! (William Edwards' collection)

Black Hawk gone. Rope on ground (William Edwards' collection).

putting about three or four soldiers in each. We stayed there for about an hour and a half and then went back to our daily business. The intention was to show that we could conduct a rapid reinforcement of the compound if necessary and the detainees were all lined up outside their tents watching this. That's the effect we wanted. The detainees would then pass out the information of what we did on that day to their loved ones and comrades on the outside, which we would then intercept. Things like the number of towers, number of guards in the towers, what kind of weapons were being held. This was designed to change all that, causing the enemy to delay and reassess their plans.

"After, our brigade commander asked, 'Did you achieve the desired effect?' I replied, 'We certainly got their attention.'"

17

It's Good to Talk

"Technology is a word that describes something that doesn't work yet."—Douglas Adams

While in Balad, the battalion didn't have the ability to call their families who were back in Germany. Major Edwards recalled how a fortuitous visit to Kuwait provided an essential communications bridge: "Before then, we didn't have any consistency to get word back, simply because we didn't have the infrastructure. So, here's what happened.

"I was coming back from Kuwait in September 2003, and I was trying to procure some parts for our vehicles. There was an equipment area in Kuwait where you could go and try to get parts for your Humvees, your 5-ton trucks, or whatever your vehicle was at the time. I'd have to do some negotiating to get whichever parts we needed to keep our equipment operational, but you could usually source what you needed. I was coming back on that same RC-12 again and landed at night at the airfield in Balad. When I landed, I took the path that I normally took from the airfield back to the tactical operation center, but it had changed, because I'd been gone for three days and in those three days an Air Force unit had come into Balad and occupied the space between the airfield and the battalion headquarters.

"If you can visualize, when I left, I walked from the headquarters to the airfield unobstructed. But when I landed, there was barbed wire, new tents and all kinds of vehicles in my way. It was nighttime, no light and I was trying to navigate my way back and I ran into this Air Force unit that had comms capability outside of Iraq. I started talking to one of the young airmen and said, 'I'm trying to make my way back to that water tower over there, how do I do that? It seems you guys have it blocked all the way.' He says, 'There's a space in the concertina wire where I can open it up for you. I said, 'Great. Thank you. What kind of unit are you guys?' He replied, 'we're a combat communications unit.' I then thought, 'Hmmm,' and said, 'Do you guys know how to call Germany and the United States?' He said, 'Yes. If you ran a wire over here and plugged it into our network, that would give you guys the ability to have a phone line back to wherever you are from.' I said, 'We're a Germany based unit' and he said, 'We can definitely do that.'

"I went back to the battalion, grabbed a hold of the communications officer and said, 'can you guys get some phone wire and a phone and run it over to this unit, plug it in and run it back to the battalion, so we can set up a phone line back to Germany. He says, 'Sure. We can figure that out.' It was about 1,200 meters, which is quite a distance, and we soon learned some lessons.

"They ran the wire and had this pink phone which they had brought from Germany. They put it on the desk in the tactical operations center, which is where myself and Bob were. Initially they ran all the wire above ground, but every time a vehicle ran over the phone cable, the phone would cut out. So what they did was, they got really creative and ran it through the sewers.

"Now we had a phone, we had to establish some rules. From 10 pm to about 4 am was the call period. People could sign up to ten minutes in the unit and try to dial back to home. It was really good for morale initially, but then what happened was, we had a line of people all night long outside the tactical operations center waiting for their time to call, which is something we had to keep under control."

LTC Walters added: "This is another point about the caliber of the officers in the unit who would take initiative. Bill's making his way through barbed wire in the middle of the night and strikes up a conversation with a comms guy, a non-commissioned officer, then links up our communications officer. Nothing was easy in Iraq, so if you got the wire wrong or the comms are established and a jeep drives across and tears it all up, they had to come up with another way. There was no protocol of right or wrong. They used their initiative and through trial and error and hard work, made it function."

Edwards continued: "On another trip the following month, similar to this one I went to Kuwait for a logistics run from Balad. I flew on the RC-12 to Kuwait and spent two days acquiring needed supplies. On the way back I linked-up with two civilian aircraft maintenance guys who were contracted to go to Balad and service the RC-12 fleet. We boarded the aircraft for the night flight with our flak vest and helmet on the floor next to our seats. As we got close to Balad the pilot yelled back that we were starting our tumble, or corkscrew into the airfield. Sitting there facing each other I reached down and put on my vest and helmet. The civilian guys across from me said, 'Hey what are you doing?' and I said, 'This is the part of the flight where we get shot at.'

"They immediately scrambled to put on their helmets, however, they didn't have vests. As soon as I said we were going to get shot at, the tracers started coming at us from the ground. Tracers are bullets that are normally every fifth round in a belt that lights up so the shooter can track where they are shooting. On our approach to the airfield in Balad, we would routinely receive fire from insurgents, usually from an AK-47 machine gun or equivalent. That's why the pilots corkscrewed into the landing."

◆◆◆

Abu Ghraib prison and downtime were polar opposite terms. Anything that didn't involve incoming fire was embraced as entertainment and a time to unwind. Edwards recalled: "Back in Balad, we once got intel that the Air Force was going to drop a 500lb bomb somewhere and we wanted to see where it was going to land. So, we all went up on top of an Iraqi concrete bunker that night with lawn chairs. It was like a fireworks event."

Without proficient lines of technology, for the most part, troops were unaware of what was happening outside of their own confines. However, pre-comms, incredibly, civilians all over the world were privy to news in Iraq, while serving officers didn't know what was happening on their doorstep. A case in point is when Saddam Hussein's twelve-meter-high statue fell in Firdos Square, Baghdad, in April 2003, in the height of the invasion. Walters recalled: "We didn't have connectivity during that time and as a result didn't see any of that. There were a lot of things early on, during the initial invasion that Nancy and the families of the soldiers deployed would see back in the States or in Germany and we didn't realize it was being broadcast or anything of that nature. We were in a very tactical mode, which means we were focused on our mission and nothing else. Watching TV or any of that type of reporting was not something we were exposed to."

However, despite extremely limited access to media in Abu Ghraib, on December 13, 2003, after Saddam Hussein was captured by the 4th Infantry division, news travelled quickly to the troops. Walters added:

"The capture of Saddam Hussein was a huge morale boost to the team. When I say the team, I mean all the coalition forces that were deployed in Iraq at that time. Saddam Hussein was the main villain, the head of the enemy. He was the reason we were there. When he was captured that spurred a lot of optimism as far as, 'Hey. Okay. We did what we came for, now we can go home.' That's what soldiers look forward to. They want to complete their mission, protect their buddies and get back to their families and loved ones. A soldier is not driven by hate from those in front of him or her, soldiers are driven by love from those that are left behind them. The sooner we can do our jobs and get home is paramount to soldiers that are deployed in a combat situation. So, when Saddam Hussein was captured that was like the light at the end of the tunnel. We're getting out of here."

Unfortunately, for the 165th the fragmentary order signifying their return to Germany did not happen overnight. In the meantime, Edwards did his very best to connect the troops to the outside world: "In the beginning, at Abu Ghraib, our access to contact our families was very limited. We had already set-up an internet café in the fall of 2003 in Balad and were constantly trying to improve our position in Abu Ghraib, replicating what we'd done previously.

"After we built the infrastructure at Abu Ghraib, we set up a café in January 2004 right next to the dining facility, which gave us the capacity for outside comms. We got some Iraqi contractors to come in and build a cinderblock wall and I'll never forget it because I went into to check the quality of the work they'd carried out, because I didn't want the wall to fall in on us. It turned out it wasn't stable and was leaning, so we had to go in and reinforce it. We finally got the wall sorted out and we set up the internet café in this building. We got a satellite dish and all these things we needed to get it going. Once it was up and running, soldiers could jump on a computer and send a note home. We had it open 24/7 and it was never abused. People would go in, send their notes and move on. The facility became a great resource and was also open to the military police and the other tenant units on the base."

Through the mayor, alongside Amar and Muhamed, the battalion were able to add a brushing of luxury to what were functional, yet harsh living conditions. Edwards explained: "When we got to Abu Ghraib, our signal officer, Romeo and the mayor, said we should try to get a satellite dish and armed forces network (AFN) box for the tactical operations center, just so we could have one of the major news channels on. We

Inside Abu Ghraib

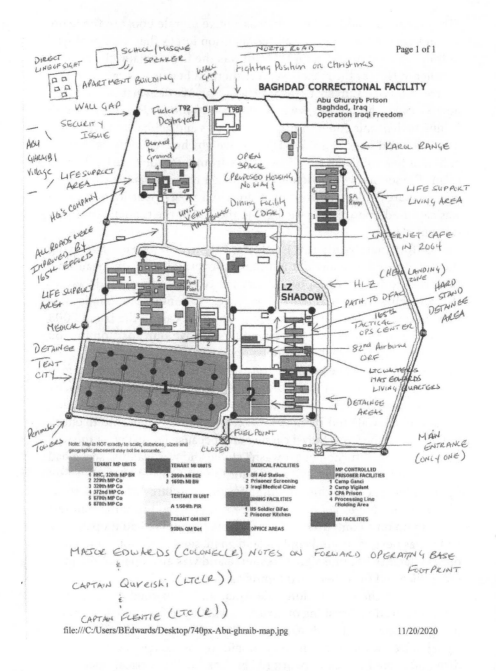

DIRECT LINE OF SIGHT

SCHOOL / MOSQUE SPEAKER

APARTMENT BUILDING

WALL GAP

NORTH ROAD

Fighting Position on Christmas

BAGHDAD CORRECTIONAL FACILITY

Abu Ghurayb Prison
Baghdad, Iraq
Operation Iraqi Freedom

WALL GAP

SECURITY ISSUE

ABU GHRAIBI Village

LIFE SUPPORT AREA

HQ's COMPANY

ALL ROADS WERE IMPROVED BY 165th EFFORTS

LIFE SUPPORT AREA

MEDICAL

DETAINEE TENT CITY

Perimeter Towers

Fucked T92 Destroyed

T98

Burned to Ground

OPEN SPACE (PROPOSED HOUSING) NO WAY!

Dining Facility (DFAC)

UNIT VEHICLE MAINTENANCE

Fuel Point

LZ SHADOW

FUEL POINT

CLOSED

KAROL RANGE

SA Range

LIFE SUPPORT LIVING AREA

INTERNET CAFE IN 2004

HLZ (HELI LANDING ZONE)

PATH TO DFAC

HARD STAND DETAINEE AREA

165th TACTICAL OPS CENTER

82nd Airborne QRF

LTC WALTERS MAJ EDWARDS LIVING QUARTERS

DETAINEE AREAS

MAIN ENTRANCE (ONLY ONE)

Note: Map is NOT exactly to scale, distances, sizes and geographic placement may not be accurate.

TENANT MP UNITS
1 HHC, 320th MP BN
2 229th MP Co
3 320th MP Co
4 372nd MP Co
5 670th MP Co
6 870th MP Co

TENANT MI UNITS
1 205th MI BDE
2 165th MI BN

TENANT IN UNIT
A 1/504th PIR

TENANT QM UNIT
938th QM Det

MEDICAL FACILITIES
1 BN Aid Station
2 Prisoner Screening
3 Iraqi Medical Clinic

DINING FACILITIES
1 US Soldier DiFac
2 Prisoner Kitchen

OFFICE AREAS

MP CONTROLLED PRISONER FACILITIES
1 Camp Ganci
2 Camp Vigilant
3 CPA Prison
4 Processing Line /Holding Area

MI FACILITIES

MAJOR EDWARDS (COLONEL (R)) NOTES ON FORWARD OPERATING BASE FOOTPRINT

&

CAPTAIN Qureishi (LTC (R))

&

CAPTAIN FLENTIE (LTC (R))

file:///C:/Users/BEdwards/Desktop/740px-Abu-ghraib-map.jpg

11/20/2020

Abu Ghraib, Nov. 2003–Feb. 2004 (William Edwards' collection).

were basically trying to create more of a connection to the outside world and some situational awareness. However, doing the simple things was often a hard task.

"One of our guys from the long-range surveillance company got wounded and was MEDEVACed. This was in the early days when if you had a slight wound, you'd get evaced, then you'd come back. Later on, you didn't come back, you were replaced, and you were allowed to recover in Germany or wherever you were sent to. I had a unit credit card for small purchases, and I gave the wounded soldier the credit card number and said, 'When you come back, bring an AFN box back with you.'

"An AFN box gave us connection to the network that was based out of Germany, although it didn't have the ability to allow us to see U.S. TV production shows or German ones at that. We had some TV capability, but it was really weird European channels.

"So, the soldier came back and brought the AFN box back, which he bought at the post exchange. Through Muhamed and Amar, we acquired a satellite dish and all the cabling off the local economy. All we had to do now was set the dish up.

"We were running the cables from the TV to the satellite dish and up to the roof of this textile factory warehouse where we were living and working in. The communications officer and his guys now had the task of making the satellite dish and network box work.

"They had little walkie talkies and it was really comical. They had a private first-class soldier, who was straight out of Basic and AIT on the roof of the building and they were talking to him via the walkie talkie, getting him to move it slightly to get signal strength. 'Move a little to the left,' and he'd move it, 'No, no, no. That's too far. Move it back.' This went on for about forty-five minutes. This was great entertainment.

"This carried on until the early evening hours and all of a sudden we had incoming fire into the base. Mortars, rockets, gunfire. This soldier is still on the roof as this indirect fire comes in and he jumps off and lands in the doorway of the tactical operations center and we pulled him in by his shirt so he could come in under cover. These attacks were fast and furious, but only usually lasted about thirty seconds.

"After the incoming assault stopped, we said, 'Okay. Time to get back on the roof. We've got to get this satellite dish set up.' He looks at us in disbelief and says, 'I'm not going back up there!' We're like, 'It's fine. Get back up there.' 'I almost got killed up there!' he replies. We finally got him back on the roof and the communications officer and his guys ended up getting the connection made."

Once connected to the outside world, the content certainly provided entertainment. Major Edwards recalled: "AFN was a private network for the military families all over the world. They had 'infomercials' which were not normal TV commercials. These infomercials were like, 'Be careful who you're talking to,' and 'If you need fuel coupons, go to X, Y and Z.' It was really comical, and we made fun of them all the time.

"One time, we're in Abu Ghraib watching a channel and an infomercial comes up. One of the senior officers in Germany was wearing a pristine desert camouflage uniform and the latest body Armor. So, there's this guy with this great pressed uniform and we're all dirty, taking showers in a plywood room. Someone suddenly says, 'How and why does he have body Armor? He's in Germany. He doesn't even need it. We should have that body Armor!' At this time, we only had about five sets of the latest body Armor for a unit of over four hundred people. We only had the flak vests which we were deployed with, which were from the late 1960s, early '70s perhaps. They were not bullet proof or shrapnel proof, but at least something to wear. If something happened outside of the base, we would share these body Armor vests. The guys started saying, 'Turn the TV off. We don't want to see that.' It was funny. Fast forward to January though and we were able to have the Superbowl on, which was a big event for us to be a part of over in Iraq at the time."

Edwards continued: "Getting movies that we could look at during some downtime was always a plus. Especially if they were good movies and cheap. We would typically watch them in a common area, and anybody interested could sit and watch it.

"On this occasion in January 2004, I'd set myself the task of getting a movie for us all to watch. That was probably the only mission I ever gave myself! The Iraqi economy at the time could get the latest movies from Asia, or wherever, very cheaply. I picked up this movie for a dollar on my way back to Abu Ghraib after a patrol from Baghdad International Airport. It was one of those copies where some guy is filming somewhere and as he coughs his camera shakes, that sort of thing. I don't think it had even hit the U.S. yet, but then again, maybe it had, because we were super disconnected from what was going on in the U.S. and the U.K. at the time, in fact anywhere.

"I pick up this movie, return to Abu Ghraib and grabbed our

communications officer. 'Can you set up this movie in a small room and let's get everyone together.' 'No problem,' he replies.

"About twenty-five of us assemble in this plywood room in a warehouse that night and just as the movie gets going, we got hit with a mortar, or rocket fire. We took some serious indirect fire that evening. The ceiling in the building we were in started shaking and crumbling down, covering us in dust as we are all scrambling for cover getting on the floor trying to figure out what was going on.

"After a couple of minutes, we had to go into our battle drills and take accountability for the unit. Things like; do we have to call MEDEVAC helicopters, is anyone hurt, what facilities have been damaged? We got reports from the company commanders and first sergeants on status of the wounded, injured, and damage. We did have a few soldiers wounded, who caught shrapnel, which was not a good outcome for us overall.

"We're going through all of this and by this stage, your guard is up and your adrenaline is flowing. But as the expression says, 'The show must go on.' I went to the communications officer and said, 'Can you get the movie back up? We want to finish watching it.' 'No problem,' he replies.

"I went back to my area to grab something and then headed back to where the movie was being shown. When I walked in, everyone was sitting there in their flak vests and helmets. I said, 'What's going on here?' They said, 'We're going to watch the rest of the movie, but we might as well watch it prepared.' We started the movie back and watched the rest without further interruptions.

"Those are significant events when they happen, so to turn it on its head and finish the movie, but in full armor, that put a light-hearted spin on the event. It was a humorous story in some respects, but it also showed the delicacy of Abu Ghraib."

18

Under Fire

"In every battle there comes a time when both sides consider themselves beaten, then he who continues the attacks wins."—Ulysses S. Grant, 18th President of the United States

Combat deployment comes with obvious concerns. Knowing your departure date is sometimes a comforting solace for soldiers to embrace; however, the process is far from immediate. LTC Walters explained: "When we arrived in November 2003, we didn't know when we'd be replaced. What happened was, every day, Combined Joint Task Force 7 would cut a FRAGO (fragmentary order) which would be sent to me on email on a classified system and within that FRAGO, it would have different tasks for different units. You couldn't leave theater without having the authorization from that FRAGO. When that order went out, it told all the military units that were in Iraq at the time what was happening. That was important, because it lets the folks at Combat Support Center Scania know that the brigade and battalion were coming at a particular time, and they could prepare accordingly. And when Bill and Romeo started coordinating with those units, the first thing they were asked was, 'What's your authorization?' That's when you had to refer to the FRAGO. We'd say for example, 'Combined Joint Task Force 7 is directing the 205th Military Intelligence Brigade to redeploy on such and such a date.' That was our authority for us to have that convoy on the road, get gas, so everything was provided for us. So, by early January 2004 at Abu Ghraib, every day the FRAGO came in, I was updating the battalion with the same information. 'No change of mission.'"

Something else that hadn't changed around this time was the sound of explosive devices; however, on occasions, they came without malice. Edwards recalled: "What happened a lot of times is units in the area

LTC Walters briefing the troops—no change to mission (William Edwards' collection).

of operation, and I think in this case it was the First Armored Division, they were going to do a controlled blast of former Russian BM-21, 122mm rockets, really big ammunitions. They'd dig holes in the ground, attach charges to it, stay a safe distance away and then blew these up so they couldn't be used against us in any form.

"This particular evening, I was getting ready to watch a DVD on my laptop and this massive explosion goes off and throws me out of the cot. I was like, 'What the hell?' I went into the tactical operation center, and everyone was shocked. They didn't know if it was another mortar attack, or rocket attack on the base, but it wasn't. We ended up getting on the radios to figure out what was going on, because we hadn't been told what was going to happen. They probably should have put out a FRAGO from the corps letting us know at what time and location, and that it was a controlled explosion."

One particular explosion around this time, however, was by no means a controlled exercise. Edwards recalled: "Every day we had mortar attacks, but on this day we had around forty incoming

120mm mortars and Chinese rockets in about 90 seconds. It was one of those things where you might have been thinking about going to get a cup of coffee or something and next thing, bang, bang, bang and the mortars were coming in one after the after."

Walters added: "Everything happened really fast, and we had to react just as quick. One of the first things we had to do was report to higher headquarters that we were under attack. The radio operator in the tactical operations center called the brigade and they acknowledged that and helped to provide a follow up. But we had to wait for the incoming fire to stop before we could go to the tactical operations center or entry control point, or a tower, because, when those things hit, shrapnel goes 360 degrees, and you can really take a severe injury if you are not careful. In the follow up, we describe the event and any further enemy activity, which included casualties, specific weapons used by the enemy and damage to the forward operating base."

Unfortunately, casualties did occur on this occasion. Edwards explained: "Most people were able to be treated, even though they had shrapnel in their body, but one soldier was MEDEVACed. One of our admin clerks took some shrapnel in his leg. I went to see him because he had been administered by the medics on site, but we kept him at Abu Ghraib, because it wasn't life threatening. I went to see him in his living area and he was lying in bed in pain. That's my key memory, post mortar attack."

The casualties were not exclusive to the 165th. Edwards continued: "As we were doing casualty evacuation from the base, some of the detainees were killed that night. I don't know the numbers, because our mission wasn't detainee operations, but they were living in tents in the open space and when these mortars came in there were people walking outside, going from one spot to another, going to the bathroom, whatever it was. Those casualties would have fallen under the military police who would have treated the wounded and dealt with the remains of those that were killed. The forward operating base was so small, that any type of ordnance that was going to land in that space was going to affect someone in some form or fashion."

Walters added: "If those concrete buildings weren't there for the soldiers, we would have been digging fighting positions. We would have set up sleeping areas with sandbags and overhead cover, with sandbags on top. The U.S. Army would have taken those force protection measures necessary to protect their soldiers, given the fact they were getting shot at. If indirect fire was coming in, at least people had a place to run to and get under cover."

After reading out 'No change of mission,' for over a month, Walters finally had the pleasure of delivering a new narrative: "I addressed the unit and said, 'We have a change in mission. Let your family know we are coming home.' As you can imagine, everyone was very happy. If they had the means to communicate with their family and loved ones at that moment, they were doing that. That's one of the things about the order is that it allows the soldiers to know what they can and cannot share with their family members. Leaving Iraq in February was not going to be an operational security matter, so it was fine for them to share this information.

"Our replacement unit was coming from Fort Gordon, Georgia. They knew they were going to be in Iraq, but as far as where they were going to be in Iraq, my guess is that they wouldn't have found out immediately that they were coming to Abu Ghraib. We had to go through the transition of authority, then went into the detail and the date of redeployment and what the battalion's responsibilities were. That's when the staff at the battalion level, under Bill's direction went into that planning process. Then the ops officer cut the order which outlined the specified tasks they needed to accomplish. The company then did their own mission analysis to see what the change of mission and specified tasks were and in turn briefed that to all their personnel. What happened after that, especially after a change of mission, was the subordinate commanders came back and provided a brief back to me, saying, this is how they were going to execute the redeployment and what their plan was. I then had to go to the brigade and brief the brigade commander on how the battalion was going to conduct this redeployment."

Edwards added: "That whole process also happened in Balad when we had a change of mission to come to Abu Ghraib, although that one happened a lot faster. It wasn't anything new to me because I'd been practicing that all the time in Germany. The process is pretty much inherent to military and tactical leadership. Walking the steps from change of mission, to issuing orders, to executing orders. My very first assignment as an Armor officer, I did rail operations in my sleep. Of a thirty-year career for me, at least fifteen were in deployments or training, so we became very proficient. I measured up the size of the task and the timeframe to execute it and got on with it.

"The replacing unit after the fragmentary order was issued was coming from the States, so that was a big move and took time. They had to get ready training wise, shipping equipment etc, from the States. In those days, units were bringing equipment with them. It wasn't worked out at that point where you walked in and fell in on equipment, which did happen later on. That was called, theater provided equipment.

"For the majority of the soldiers, getting the news of returning home was almost a euphoric moment. For me, I went from obviously being happy to straight away thinking, 'Okay. We've got to pick up the pace a little bit.' I got the staff together and said, 'We need to kick into high gear. We've got a lot of stuff to do between now and then.'

"As the executive officer, I had to ensure my chain of command was fully functional. After myself, there was the operations officer, the command sergeant major, the company commanders, first sergeants and then the chain of command goes all the way down to the most junior soldiers. In addition, I was also responsible for transitioning our replacements, including my incoming executive officer. My job during this period was making sure the soldiers were resourced, making sure they were functioning, had ammunition, had chow, maintenance repair parts, etc. When we got the change of mission order to go to Kuwait, the focus was now a full-on 500km logistics operation."

◆◆◆

Abu Ghraib's volatility by now had become a norm, but unfortunately, the surrounding geography outside of the prison was just as unforgiving. Edwards explained: "Romeo was the patrol leader with a second lieutenant and what happened on this day turned out to be one of those pinnacle events for us as a unit.

"As we were getting ready to redeploy the battalion in the coming weeks, we knew that a unit was assigned to come in and replace us. My job as the executive officer was to check all the conditions so that Bob and our operations officer, could get the battalion moved to Kuwait and we could start processing our vehicles and get our equipment back to Germany.

"I started talking to the logistics staff of the battalion about starting to send equipment home that we were not using. At the time there were a lot of Air Force C5 and C17 vessels that were coming into theater bringing equipment but were leaving empty. A friend of mine said, 'You might want to think of using some of these C17's to get your stuff back early,' and that's exactly what we did. We took the initiative to lessen our load and started packing the extra equipment we weren't using or didn't need into these military conexes, then taking them to Baghdad, loading them on the empty Air Force airplanes and then flying them back to Germany.

"Romeo was running combat patrols between Abu Ghraib and Baghdad, specifically Baghdad International Airport, and had done this convoy on numerous occasions and was always well prepared."

Captain Romeo Qureishi explained the relevance of that all-important preparation: "When you come under fire, it's always a surprise, but you prepare yourself on every convoy for something like that to happen. For every convoy that took say fifteen minutes, it took about three hours to prepare between vehicles, equipment and personnel. Then thirty minutes before we went out on that convoy, we would go through 'Actions on the Objective,' which allowed for contingencies, in case something were to happen. Things like vehicle breakdown or an attack. We also had a check list we went over called pre combat inspection, making sure we had enough fuel, ammo and that our weapons were ready.

"The whole 165th Battalion had been there since Thanksgiving, but despite being under attack every day in Abu Ghraib, at that point we'd never been hit or shot at doing these convoys. However, one thing I always emphasized to the convoy was, 'We can get hit at any time. You need to be prepared. There's not going to be some guy standing up like an easy static target on the shooting range. They'll be hidden behind vegetation or some big obstacle. In the possibility of an attack, you return fire and you suppress as much fire as you can. Any flashes means that's gun fire coming at you. Any smoke trails means someone is firing a rocket propelled grenade at you. These are things the guys remembered on the day. Whether it was me or somebody else who was the convoy commander, the team knew what they had to do in any of those situations. The plan was well thought through and we had secondary and tertiary fallback positions."

Edwards added: "When you talk in terms of secondary and tertiary, that's more equated to a defense. You have a defense as your primary fighting position, a secondary or a fallback position, you may have a tertiary or third fallback position depending on the pressure from the enemy. You have that planned out. In an operational move, you're focused more on battle drills. You don't have set positions, because you are moving. In this case we were executing a combat patrol movement. Romeo would have been acting on a battle drill and not a set position."

Walters commented: "Once we started getting hit with IEDs, we were trying to come up with ways to mitigate the risk. One of the things we often did when our convoy had to stop prior to its final destination, was 'fives and twenty-fives,' and here's why. If an IED went off, a convoy would come to a standstill and pull over to the shoulder of the road, while they were treating any of the wounded soldiers that were struck with the IED. In the meantime, recovery would come to retrieve the vehicle. Meanwhile, all those other vehicles in the convoy would be parked on the side of the road.

"The standard operating procedure was to do a 360-degree security check of five meters from the vehicle and then from five meters out to twenty five meters, looking for IEDs. There would usually be multiple IEDs lined up, but the insurgents would only initiate one. Then while the convoy was dealing with that, they would detonate the others when everyone was outside of their vehicles, looking to cause maximum damage to the soldiers.

"Romeo was our logistician leading these convoys, as well as being a soldier and a leader. Counter insurgencies are definitely a different kind of warfare. It changes the definition and the battlefield framework. You don't have a deep area, a close fight, a support area or a sustainment area. It's a very fluid battlefield and you can get hit anytime, anywhere, even right outside the entry control point."

Captain Qureishi recalled this particular convoy from February 2004: "Under the direction of LTC Walters and Major Edwards, we wanted to get as much of our equipment back to Germany as soon as possible and doing that by air was the fastest option.

"We were on a routine convoy to Baghdad International Airport, a route we would do at least twice a week, because there was very little in Abu Ghraib, so, logistically, we depended on a lot of things that came out of the airport. You could also call it the admin/log convoy, because of the administrative personnel who would come with us to pick up mail.

"We were fortunate for the most part on Main Supply Route, Tampa, but on that day our luck changed. I was convoy commander of ten vehicles, and we had three checkpoints between Abu Ghraib and the airport and they were all easily identifiable. When you are going from point A to point B, the Army teaches you to do map reconnaissance of where you are going, and you'll pick out specific places on a map and label that a specific checkpoint. These were usually terrain features or something on the road that would indicate we were on the right track.

"Between Abu Ghraib and the airport, there were three overpasses, so we made them the checkpoints. Checkpoint 1 was the overpass closest to Abu Ghraib and checkpoint 3 was approximately two kilometers from the airport, opposite a small town. To get to the airport from the highway, you took a sharp left at checkpoint 3, driving northeast, also known as the dog leg into the airport. An additional note: passing through the overpasses was quite nerve wracking as, at the time, the insurgents liked to use overpasses as locations where to emplace IEDs."

Edwards added: "You were vulnerable to anything being dropped from up above. One of the things we did as part of the tactics, techniques and procedures framework from Abu Ghraib to Baghdad International Airport, was when going under the overpass, to continuously switch lanes, so our movements weren't predictable. There was also another issue. The Iraqis were using cars to get in front of our patrols to slow them down, to get us into a kill zone. If you had an Iraqi vehicle get in front of your lead vehicle and they significantly slowed down, that was an indication from our perspective that we either needed to ram that car and get it off road, get around it quickly or take some other form of action to negate the threat."

Qureishi continued: "On this morning, most of the convoy had already taken the dog leg left at Checkpoint 3 and were heading toward the back gate at Baghdad International Airport. I was convoy commander in the lead vehicle, which meant I was already about five hundred meters past that checkpoint. If there was a place you were going to get hit, it was there, because you went from driving at about 65–70mph to the whole convoy slowing down to a virtual standstill. That was something we called a fatal funnel within that ambush, which is something we discussed with the soldiers and non-commissioned officers all the time to make them aware when entering the zone.

"Suddenly, I got a call saying we'd been hit with a complex ambush (when you have more than one type of incoming enemy fire, whether that's IED, rocket propelled grenades or small arms fire) from the right-hand side, at the exact same place where Kasem Soleimani was killed on January 3, 2020. What surprised me with this ambush was that the insurgents were shooting into the town, which told me they were probably not from there. The attackers were set up about a hundred to one hundred and fifty meters away and were camouflaged by tall grass.

"I didn't notice us getting shot at, but I soon realized something was wrong as our last two vehicles slowed down significantly. We lost track of the trail vehicle (the last vehicle of the convoy) because I found out that the second to last vehicle, which was a M923 5-Ton 6x6 cargo truck, had been hit and couldn't move.

"The reason why the 5-ton was disabled, was because it took a rocket propelled grenade round to the airbrake cylinder. Incredibly, the round didn't go off, but just got stuck in the airbrake. The driver tried to move forward but the vehicle could only move backwards. We only found out later on about the grenade when the explosive ordnance experts came over to the airport to deal with that unexploded ammunition, which was pretty frightening. The good thing about that is they always talk about how a lot of the inventory of the Iraqi Army was very old. Well, the grenade that hit us was one of the old ones, so it didn't detonate. However, at the time, I didn't realize the damage, so I said, 'Just leave the vehicle there. We'll take care of it later. Just get out of the kill zone.'

"I called for the trail vehicle which was with the lieutenant. The gunner and lieutenant went back to get two personnel from the 5-ton truck. At this point it was all hands on deck. We had a chaplain who would normally go on these trips, and I'd tell him, 'Whether we are going or coming back, now's not the time to close your eyes and rest. While you cannot carry a weapon because you are a chaplain, you need to tell us where the shots are coming from.' He wasn't with us that day, but that gives you an idea of the emphasis of how important everybody was whenever we did this convoy. Also, it's worth noting that the soldiers in the convoy were totally familiar with firing weapons as we were always practicing on the ranges, so when they had to do it for real, they were prepared. However, for many in the convoy, on that day it was their first time firing weapons in a combat situation. When they started firing, clearly, their training shone through, and they were able to suppress the enemy.

"I stopped the convoy and everyone got out and started to return fire. One of the vehicles had our non-commissioned officer in charge, a young female staff sergeant and driver, a private first class. When they were stopped, they got out of the vehicle and one said, 'Captain Qureishi said to fire at any flashes or smoke trails, because we're not going to see any bad guys standing up.' That day, she fired her full load, which was two hundred and ten rounds. There was brass everywhere. That's a day I'll never forget."

18. Under Fire

Walters added a light-hearted note: "Brass casings is one definition of 'brass.' Another definition of brass is a very senior officer, because of all the brass they wear on their uniform. On this occasion, it was empty shell casings and not a bunch of generals sitting around a convoy!"

Qureishi continued: "At the end of the convoy, the trail vehicle which had the lieutenant went to go pick up the other two personnel in the disabled 5-ton vehicle, because their fire power was incapacitated. I'd lost contact with them, so I took my vehicle directly to the back, only to find out probably two or three hundred meters away the trail vehicle had caught up with the rest of the convoy.

"One of our sergeants was in a two-seater M998 Humvee, which had an M249 machine mounted in the back. The reason they couldn't contact us was because the sergeant had fired so many rounds at the enemy from his automatic weapon, that he shot off the antenna on his own vehicle. Once we consolidated and reorganized, we got accountability of everybody except the 5-ton truck. By then the quick reaction force was on its way, while the rest of us made it back to the airport. We did what we had to do and nobody was killed. The only person who was hurt was the lieutenant who needed a bit of first aid on his right hand after the glass of his Humvee shattered.

"If you are an infantry soldier, your job is to close with, maneuver and kill the enemy. Ours as combat support was to suppress the enemy, get out of the kill zone and live to fight another day. Our guys did a good enough job of suppressing fire and the evidence of blood trails showed that we did hit some of the insurgents. It was a good day for us fortunately."

A quick reaction force is an essential response unit for any combat scenario. Walters provided further detail in relation to their role: "For us, they're typically another long-range surveillance team. You'll have a long-range surveillance team that does the surveillance mission, another does the insertion and extraction with vehicles and then you have a separate element, sometimes two, depending on what the company commander deems as the minimum essential combat power needed. So, if something happens and that radio message comes to the tactical operations center, we task the quick reaction force to respond. That's what happened when Romeo was ambushed.

"I think it's also worth understanding the larger picture here. The counter insurgency which we were engaged with at that time, was not the typical type of combat. There wasn't a front line of enemy forces and everybody else was in a relatively safe zone in the rear. In a counter insurgency, everyone is a soldier and everyone is subject to being shot at and rocketed. Consequently, every soldier on the battlefield is expected to use their weapon, whatever that may be. It does not matter what their particular skill set is or their military occupational specialty.

"Romeo did a great job highlighting our female staff sergeant. She was a non-commissioned officer, who was not an infantry soldier or Armor soldier, this was a personnel specialist, who hopped out of her vehicle and started returning fire, doing multiple reloads of her weapon. That's what counter insurgencies are all about. That's the nature of that kind of warfare and that's what we were involved with."

◆◆◆

The term "under fire" can come in many guises, but the day before the 165th Battalion was getting ready to depart from Anbar to make the long journey home to Germany via Kuwait, they were literally under a blaze of fire. Major Edwards recalled: "Our replacement unit, the 203rd Military Intelligence Battalion, was on the forward operating base with us and we had done our left seat/right seat and transition of authority, which is an Army term for risk management mechanism during transition. The way it works is where another unit or person, comes in and the new person or unit shadows the outgoing unit or person around for anywhere between three to five days. The person that's outgoing would be in the left seat meaning, they are still in charge and the incoming watch what they do for the next week. Then they swap and the new guy that just got in, would do three to five days in charge with the outgoing guy watching him and making sure he's doing everything correctly, shadowing, making sure they minimize the risk of error during the transition, which is a time when errors typically go up. The impact of those errors ultimately mean that soldiers can get killed. That's why it's essential to minimize that risk during the transition.

"The 203rd were now in charge of the tactical operations center and going through all the drills, checking soldiers, going through all the proper procedures, but we were pretty much on chill out mode now as we knew we were heading home. That evening I was in my little sleeping area relaxing when we got mortared in the forward operating base and I can immediately remember thinking two things, 'I hope nobody is hurt and I can't wait to get out of Abu Ghraib!' We all ran into the tactical operations center to see what was going on. The incoming battalion commander, who was replacing Bob, also came with us.

"We were up in the northwest corner of Abu Ghraib and there were some buildings where the headquarters and headquarters service company lived and it was also where our motor pool and maintenance was carried out. We also had all of our conexes, storage containers and equipment there.

"The journey from Abu Ghraib to Kuwait was about 800km and I needed the capability to refuel our vehicles. We had a 5-ton fueler truck which we called a tank and pump unit and that acted as our reserve fuel source, because, as much as you told soldiers before leaving, 'Wash your windshields, top up your fuel, top up your fluids,' there was always going to be someone who would stop and say, 'Hey, Sir. I'm out of gas!'

"We had built berms all around the fueler and the thought was, if a mortar or rocket hit, the berms would block the shrapnel. The only way it wasn't going to be protected is if there was a direct hit and that's exactly what happened that night. The mortar landed right on top of it. The flames were a couple of hundred feet in the air and we were standing there with amazement as this thing was burning to the ground.

"Bob was standing there alongside LTC Edwards, myself and all of the soldiers out of their buildings watching this truck burn to the

Under fire. The 5-ton fuel truck after the mortar attack (William Edwards' collection).

ground. The first thing we did was to get everyone back inside, because you never knew when the next round of artillery could be and everyone was out in the open as prime targets. As we are looking at this inferno, Bob leant over to me and said, 'Hey Bill, we need a plan. We've got to figure out how to replace this. That was our emergency fuel for our road march.' Then the incoming battalion commander said, 'Bill. I'm real sorry this happened to you guys.'

"Suddenly, one of the company commanders comes up to me and says, 'Sir, the fuel truck driver wants to speak to you.' The soldier walks over, who turned out to be the fueler driver for our battalion. I said, 'What's up?' and he replied, 'Sir. That's not our fuel truck.' I said, 'What do you mean?' He said, 'Sir. We've been here for months. I moved our truck to those buildings over there and hid it.'

"In brief, the 203rd had moved their fueler into the parking spot which got mortared. I leant over to my replacement and said, 'I don't know how to tell you this, but that's not our fueler. That's yours.' He said, 'What? That's my fueler?'"

Walters recalled: "The incoming commander and I in the evenings would go and grab a cup of coffee and start talking through various issues that I felt I needed to share to help posture him for success. We were having one of those conversations when this incident occurred. We then moved down to the location where the tanker was and we were standing there watching those flames go way up into the sky. It was a dark night, which made the fire stand out even more.

"When the little discussion took place about who owned the fueler, he and I both moved forward, shielded our eyes from the flames so we could read the bumper number to sort out any confusion. On Army vehicles, you have a stenciled number on the bumper to let you know which company and battalion owns that vehicle. We got up there, read the number and I had a tremendous feeling of relief once I saw it was not a 165th truck. I felt bad about it, but on a trip of that length, anything can go wrong and that would be the only way to top up vehicles once you've exhausted your five-gallon cans. The alternative was getting a tow bar on the exhausted vehicle, because you wouldn't want to leave it stranded in the middle of the desert."

Edwards continued: "The new commander had an executive officer and he started yelling for him because that new executive officer was going to have to figure out how to fix the situation. I said, 'Sir, it's not a big deal. You guys have plenty of time to fix it.' What I did that night with my replacement was give him some help and gave him some contacts at the airport and in the Baghdad area to get it sorted out."

Walters added: "I did say to my replacement, 'I can leave my tank and pump unit with you,' and to his credit he said, 'No. You're going to need that for the convoy.' He'd just brought his battalion up, so he knew what the requirements were for us to convoy back to Kuwait. Everything was manageable, but I'm just glad it wasn't our task to manage. By this stage, we just wanted to head home."

19

So Long Abu Ghraib

"Now get the hell out of here and go change the world."
—Lucille Ball

After surviving a complex ambush and a close call with an incinerated 5-ton fuel tanker, the time had come to bid Abu Ghraib prison farewell. In addition to the mental pictures every soldier and detainee walked away with, Major Edwards had also taken some photographs which he fully intended developing: "I had a bunch of those disposable box cameras that were covered in cardboard, to capture things we were doing and to give a flavor of Abu Ghraib. Shortly before leaving, I had taken pictures of the gallows, the holding cells and the area of the hallways when you walked in, which was really eerie. The gallows is one of those places that you went inside once to see how they were constructed and how they operated, then once you'd seen them, there was no real attraction to go back in. The hooks on the ceiling still remained and the trapdoors beneath those being hanged were in full sight. Occasionally, when visitors would come to the forward operating base, depending on who was hosting the visit, either the military police or ourselves would take them there so they could see the notorious gallows which were run under the rule of Saddam Hussein.

"So, the day we were leaving Abu Ghraib, we were standing in the main area getting our vehicle serials set up and I took the camera from my rucksack and put it under the wheel of the Humvee. As we drove out of there I forgot about the camera and that was the end of my photos!"

Opposite top: **Major Edwards observing the cells which had been used for detainees on death row in Abu Ghraib.** *Opposite bottom:* **The trapdoor which was released beneath the hanging prisoner. Note Major Edwards' left hand, holding the disposable camera which never made it back home (Mike Flentie's collection)**

19. So Long Abu Ghraib

Inside Abu Ghraib

Spine-chilling photo of the hanging area of the gallows. Note the hooks in the ceiling above trapdoors where the prisoners would be hung from the necks (Mike Flentie's collection).

Leaving Abu Ghraib and taking the convoy on a two-day road trip to Kuwait was a mission in itself. Edwards explained: "We had six serials of about twenty vehicles per serial to transport a battalion of four hundred soldiers. We tactically split the routes up in order to reduce the probability of us being easy targets, but had an agreed midway point called Combat Support Center Scania, which was about 400km away in southern Iraq, near Nasiriyah. It was kind of like the refueling and rest point before you made the journey into Kuwait.

"The serials started pulling up in pretty good time around early evening. We kept everyone in their serials, lined them up next to each other and then said, 'Get some food and sleep,' because we wanted our drivers fresh. It was all about getting home safely at this point. However, Romeo and his serial didn't turn up and I was frankly, more than a little bit concerned.

"Once you're on those roads and it gets dark, that's when it gets difficult. I didn't have comms with him, and I was very worried because I thought they were either lost or had been ambushed. Also, from a

158

logistics perspective, their break in contact could potentially hold up the movement."

Captain Romeo Qureishi explained what had transpired: "As the battalion logistics officer, I was convoy commander of the sixth and final serial. The battalion convoy left early in the morning with a staggered time between each serial. While we planned to make it to Scania during daylight hours, we arrived much later because we took a different route from the other serials, and we were slowed down by traffic in at least two cities. Despite arriving in the early hours of the morning, members of the sixth serial got a meal and at least six hours of sleep. As a result, we were ready to convoy later that morning, with a rejuvenated sense of purpose as we were on our way to Kuwait to redeploy home."

Edwards continued: "We stayed at Scania briefly overnight, changed our drivers and then, due to the tight schedule we were on, continued heading south to Kuwait. The first step we called getting out of the Ring of Cancer, or what many referred to as the Sunni Triangle of Death. The second leg of the trip was to Camp Doha, Kuwait which was about 450km away and although it was nowhere near as hostile as the previous leg, we would constantly remind each other to be cognizant at all times.

"The crossing point into Kuwait from Iraq was Camp Navistar, which was in a border town called Abdali. We spent about half a day here with an Army reserve logistical unit who were waiting for us, to help us transition our equipment. One of their jobs was to pick up the ammunition, take it away and basically take care of all the administration and logistics involved with that process."

You can take the soldiers out of Abu Ghraib, but you can't take the Abu Ghraib out of the soldiers. Edwards gleefully recalled: "The day before we were getting ready to pull out of Abu Ghraib, I was talking to the ops sergeant major, the same guy who was dressed in the Santa suit on Christmas Day, and I said, 'Let's get the word out that we should only take our personal basic load of ammunition on this trip out of Iraq.' What that meant was about six or seven magazines for our rifles, a certain amount of 50 caliber ammunition and maybe some hand grenades. The reason we wanted to keep it minimal is because we wanted to leave our ammunition stock for the unit that was coming in to replace us. They had their own basic load, but we were going to leave ours, so they had more than enough for their tour. The ops sergeant major said, 'No problem sir. Got it.'

Inside Abu Ghraib

"So, here we are at Navistar the crossing point into Kuwait. On arrival at Abu Ghraib we'd put steel all over our trucks to up Armor them and sandbags inside and were trying to remove that and get them into a state that was similar to what we took them into Iraq. I was sitting in the vehicle commander seat of my Humvee taking a nap when I hear this knock on the side of the door. I woke up and said, 'What's up Master Sergeant?' and he said, 'Sir, I need a couple of 5-ton trucks.' I replied, 'What do you need 5-tons for?' and he says, 'Well, we've got to put all the ammo in it.' I said, 'I thought I told you guys, just bring personal basic load.' He says, 'We brought everything. We heard you, but we weren't taking any chances!' If something had happened during that journey, I guess, without a doubt, we were ready.

"He is one of those characters you don't forget. He was a good soldier, but he was also funny as hell. After we got back, I didn't see him until 2010 and when I did, it was as if he picked up from where he'd left off. What happened was, I was back in Iraq, but this time as battalion commander, operating out of Tallil airbase and Camp Bucca at the same time, which were separated by about 400km, so it was a little bit challenging. Luckily, one of the deputy commanding general's from the 1st Infantry Division would always loan me his aircraft.

"I was coming back from Bucca and I got back to Tallil, which is just south of Nasiriyah. I was picked up at where the Black Hawk landed at the airfield, and they drove me back to the battalion headquarters and I walked into this little makeshift office I had. On the desk was a note written in pencil, which said, 'Hey sir. It's your old ops sergeant major. Where the hell are you? I'm at the airfield, I'm flying out of here.' I immediately went to my driver and said, 'Take me to the airfield right now.' Off we go to the airfield and there was basically a bunch of soldiers sitting around on their rucksacks waiting for their aircraft and then there was a room at the back which was designated for high rank officers. It was like a VIP room.

"I walked into this area, and I yelled for him and I heard, 'Who the hell's calling my name?' Classic for this guy, finding himself a couch and a place to kick his feet up. I go back there, and we hug each other. He was a civilian at this point, working in Iraq as a camera repairman, repairing surveillance cameras. I said, 'What are you doing in the VIP lounge?' and he replied, 'This is the best place to sit.' We both started laughing. There we were sitting on some couches, and I stayed with him for about an hour until his aircraft came in to leave. That's the last time I saw him.

19. So Long Abu Ghraib

"Back to Navistar. After leaving there we continued the movement to Camp Doha, which was another couple of hours further into Kuwait. When we got to Doha, we were given a warehouse to live in and we put every soldier from the battalion in the warehouse, cot to cot. It was non-stop busy and most of my time was spent with Romeo and the admin folks. The reason why I told him to go get trained on all those systems before heading to Iraq, was for this reason. TC-AIMS (Transportation Coordinators Automated Information for Movements System) was a software program we used to tag vehicles and an essential part of our systems.

When we walked into those logistics units, we could tell them, here's our TC-AIMS reports, and they could start tagging our equipment quickly in order for it to be shipped. No tag, no shipment. Romeo and I spent a tremendous amount of time working with the Army logistics systems, to make sure that what we were shipping back was based off of our MTOE. In a combat zone, the combat commander can write off specific equipment as a combat loss and then the Army will generate, off of your MTOE, a replacement for that equipment. Without that, there was no accountability. Units who were unprepared and didn't understand the systems, sometimes got stuck in Kuwait another two weeks and there was no way that was going to happen on my watch."

LTC Walters added "For me, the first day I arrived in Kuwait I was in the provost marshal's office being grilled by the 15–6 investigation team. More about that later. In the meantime, Bill was in charge of cleaning and preparing all of our vehicles to meet German agricultural standards in order to be able ship them home. The bar which the Germans maintained in terms of vehicle cleanliness was exhaustively high. Just think, after cleaning the vehicles, they would then be placed on a ship and would get salt water and dust on them, before being driven from Belgium to Germany. Didn't make sense.

"In addition to vehicle preparation, we had to get our soldiers ready for immigration and customs. That involved the soldiers laying out all their stuff and we had to identify any contraband that didn't have authorization. For example, you could get Cuban cigars in Iraq and Kuwait, which is fine to smoke them while you are there, but you couldn't take them back to Germany and certainly not to the United States. So, before we left Kuwait to get back on the plane to go to Germany, we had to do a shake down in Camp Doha and check the soldiers for Cuban cigars. If they were non–Cuban, it was okay. We just wanted to make sure our soldiers didn't get in trouble."

Qureishi added: "I'll never forget when our contractor Muhamed and his interpreter gave me four or five coins that were made of brass with Saddam's marks on them. I didn't take them because we simply weren't allowed to take any of that stuff. The only thing you could take back, were items that were going to be placed in a museum or similar and you would always need documentation to go with the items to verify their existence. This was all done to keep the integrity of the unit."

Back to vehicle preparation, Edwards recalled: "You are never supposed to mix uniforms and there's a picture of me where I'm wearing a desert jacket and green pants. That was at the wash rack, where all the vehicles went before having to pass a level of inspection and being shipped back to Germany. It was going to take around ten force ships to take them back to Antwerp and then we were going to have to rail and convoy all the equipment from Belgium to our base in Germany. The wash rack was actually at a Kuwaiti commercial facility and they had given us that space to be able to clean our vehicles, trailers, you name

Major Edwards, leading the battalion's redeployment efforts in non-matching uniform, in preparation for customs inspections of equipment returning to Germany (William Edwards' collection).

it. It was all hands on deck for two weeks solid. A couple of minutes before that picture was taken, I was under a truck with a huge power hose cleaning dirt.

"We cleaned the trucks, then they got them inspected and if they weren't happy, they'd tell you to send it back to the wash rack. You'd drive back, clean it some more and this went on and on until you saw all the vehicles lined up, certified and good to go. Then you tag them and get them ready to go on a ship in the port of Shuaiba.

"So, the vehicles were clean and tagged and we got to the port of Shuaiba with all of our rolling stock, which was over two hundred items, including all the trucks and trailers. We now needed to move our vehicles into the containment area, so we could start loading them onto the ships. We were parked on the side of the highway in the middle of the night with the entire battalion and we're trying to get into the port of Shuaiba. I went up to the entrance gate and there was a Kuwaiti national who ran the entrance to the port and I couldn't convince him to let us in.

"I grabbed Romeo, who has a great personality and I said, 'See if you can talk that guy into letting us into the port of Shuaiba.' Romeo, goes up to the entrance and I go back to my truck. Time goes by, maybe an hour and Romeo hasn't come back yet. I walk back up to the entrance of the port and I look into the little window and there's Romeo, sitting laid back with his shirt off, wearing his t-shirt, sitting on the floor having some chai tea and having a conversation with this Kuwaiti guy! Romeo looks up, sees me at the window and shoos me away."

Qureishi recalled: "I'm not a white American, if you will, and my last name is Qureishi. If you are familiar with the Middle East, the prophet Muhammad was a Qureishi and once they saw my name on my uniform, I used that to my advantage. Combine that with a bit of Arabic I'd learned over the years and that all helped for the initial introductions. So, when I sat down and told them what we were trying to do, they offered me tea and we had a long and pleasant conversation." Edwards added: "And that's how we got the battalion into the port of Shuaiba!"

Edwards continued: "Back to the convoy. We were making final preparations to leave, and I had to get the buses from Camp Wolf to transport the soldiers to their air point of debarkation. Nobody was available so I went into the big warehouse we were at and yelled out to hundreds of people, 'Hey. I need a driver who can take me to Camp Wolf. Anyone ever been there?' This guy from the long-range surveillance company says, 'Sir. I've been to Camp Wolf. I'll go with you.' I said,

'Great. By the way, you can't leave Camp Doha without a weapon.' They would actually check you had a weapon on the way out to make sure you had the ability to defend yourself.

"The distance from Doha to Wolf was about twenty miles and took roughly twenty-five minutes. I went and got a little Peugeot truck we could drive with, and I said, 'I'll drive and you ride, because you know Camp Wolf. He said, 'Sounds good.' So, it's just me and him in the truck and we are going down to Wolf to get the buses. We get out the gate in Doha and are hauling down the highway and I said to the guy, 'What exit do I get off at?' He said, 'I don't know where Camp Wolf is at sir. You just asked me if I knew of Camp Wolf.' I said, 'So you don't know how to get there?' 'That's correct Sir.'

"Here we are in the middle of the night driving down the highway and neither of us have any idea where Camp Wolf is at. I said, 'Dude. Just look for signs for Kuwaiti International Airport,' because the airport was split into two—the commercial side and Camp Wolf. We end up getting to the airport, worked out how to get to the military side and there was Camp Wolf.

"I got into where the buses were at and there were all these drivers from places like Bangladesh, Pakistan etc, whose English wasn't the best. There were no windshields on the buses, they were filthy and just looked like a bunch of junk.

"Anyway. We got seven buses and had them all lined up behind my truck, because they had to follow me back to Doha. It was like the duck and the ducklings all the way back to the camp. I was still driving and we were going down the highway, when I took a wrong turn. All seven buses followed me down this narrow street in this Kuwaiti neighborhood and there was no way to turn around. People were out on the streets staring at us and then I heard the Velcro on the kid's gun holster pull back. I said, 'What are you doing?' He said, 'Sir, I didn't get killed in Iraq and I sure to shit ain't getting killed in Kuwait,' and he pulled out his pistol. I said, 'I can't disagree with you brother.' Although there were no hostilities in Kuwait, you had to be vigilant wherever you went in that part of the world.

"We finally managed to turn our truck around, but then we had the calamity of turning all the buses around. This was the middle of the night, and they are backing up, edging backwards and forwards, until we finally all got back on the highway and made our way back to Doha. Bob was getting everyone ready at the camp, making sure the soldiers didn't have any contraband and he asked, 'How did it go?' I replied, 'Everything went awesome. No big deal.' I never told Bob that story until getting this book together.

"As a side note–Camp Wolf had the best dining facility I'd ever been in, during the entire time I was downrange. They had a full-on bakery going and you could order sandwiches. The guys would be like, 'Hey sir. Can we go to Camp Wolf for lunch?' Sometimes I would take a civilian truck and take Romeo or Mike Flentie down to Camp Wolf or a Kuwaiti naval base to eat lunch if we had time. It was a good way to keep the guys motivated and see a different scene."

Walters reflected: "Everything happens in a very deliberate fashion when you are going through redeployment. You can't start sending manpower back, because you need all those soldiers to clean the vehicles to standard. The good thing about it is that there's a discernible difference as far as they are much more relaxed, because nobody was shooting at them and there were no IEDs between Camp Doha and the assembly area where we were putting our vehicles at. But most importantly, at that stage, everybody knew they were going home, which created a totally different atmosphere with the troops.

"However, despite wanting to get home, you still had to follow what the logistics guys tell you. You may be ready by day fifteen but may not have a port date until day twenty six, so you just waited. You did physical training, you got to go to the dining facility, you wrote letters home and hopefully stayed out of trouble. As soldiers over there, we were restricted as to where we could go. Even when Bill went down there to pick up stuff when we were in Abu Ghraib, he was not able to hop in a cab and go cruising through Kuwait City, go to restaurants and hotels. That was the same for most of the soldiers. The only ones to really have the freedom to move around Kuwait City were military people who worked at the embassy.

"Kuwait City at this point had healed from the Desert Shield and Desert Storm, Gulf War tragedy and was now a metropolitan environment. The citizens were enjoying life, despite this war that was happening just to the north of their country. The Kuwaiti government was very supportive of our efforts, but they did not want to have the appearance of an occupied country, so, we were restricted to Camp Doha, which was on the northwest of Kuwait City, which kept visibility of the Kuwaiti support to a minimum."

Edwards continued: "I was working with the Air Force, preparing the process of getting the soldiers home. Back then, I was coordinating all this on a whiteboard, using color codes with different colored pens. We'd be checking the different colors as we went along, which corresponded to different tasks.

"After we were totally set, the battalion's vehicles were waiting to go on the ships and Romeo moved himself and the soldiers to the port of Shuaiba to live. When he said, 'All the vehicles are here, I'm going home.' I said, 'Nope. You're staying here. You have to count every vehicle on the ship.' Romeo was a great guy and just said, 'Yes Sir. Whatever needs doing Sir.' We stayed until all equipment was in the staging area at the port, but Romeo kept a small team of about seven people with him to help load vehicles. While we returned to Germany in late March, Romeo returned early April. The term VANI (value added, no issues) suited him perfectly. It was no surprise that he became a company commander in the next rotation when he went to Afghanistan with the 165th."

As the battalion prepared to leave Kuwait, a certain disk which Walters had been alerted to had become the hot topic of investigation and was about to make huge waves in media circles, globally.

Romeo at the Port of Shuaiba, putting in the extra legwork to ship the battalion's equipment home (Romeo Qureishi's collection).

20

"That" Disk

"The Combined Joint Task Force Commander-7 commander requested a comprehensive and all-encompassing inquiry to make findings and recommendations concerning the fitness and performance of the 800th MP Brigade."
—Excerpt from Article 15–6 Investigation
of the 800th Military Police Brigade
(a.k.a. the Taguba Report)

The Geneva Conventions established global standards to protect the human rights of prisoners; however, under the rule of Saddam Hussein, the backbone of the Conventions were contravened emphatically. The humanitarian protocols outlined how prisoners of war must not be tortured or mistreated and they must be given suitable living conditions, in addition to an adequate amount of sustenance. Unfortunately, under the management of the 800th Military Police (MP) Brigade, a subsection of detainees received barbaric care, putting the prison at Abu Ghraib once again under the Convention's breached spotlight. As the old expression goes, "Those who do not learn from history are doomed to repeat it (George Santayana)." LTC Walters shared his observations: "I didn't know anything about the 800th. All I knew was that they were an Army Reserve unit and my first encounter with them was when we arrived in Abu Ghraib.

"I met the battalion commander and his brigade commander who was based over in Baghdad. She made a couple of visits to the forward operating base while we were there, but fairly infrequently. The Combined Joint Task Force 7 commander was the commanding general and all military units in Iraq at the time worked for him. The guy I answered to on a daily basis between me and the commanding general was my brigade commander and he was put in command of U.S. forces operating on the base at Abu Ghraib, including elements of the 800th."

Major Edwards concurred: "Same here. I'd never heard of them. My first encounter with the 800th was at the forward operating base in Abu Ghraib and my first impression wasn't that good. Let's leave it at that."

Discipline is the foundation of any military operation. Without it, a battalion and brigade will eventually rot. Page six of the 15–6 report stated:

> [The lieutenant general] cited reports of detainee abuse, escapes from confinement facilities, and accountability lapses, which indicated systematic problems within the (800th MP) Brigade and suggested a lack of clear standards, proficiency and leadership.

Walters confirmed: "That's completely accurate when referring to the 800th MP Brigade, but I'd like to add something. Most soldiers want to be doing a good job, but sometimes they make poor decisions and that's when leaders need to weigh in. The other problem was the multiple layers of operations going on. You had the security and the management of the forward operating base, the detention operation still being executed by the military police and then the interrogation operation. Not all prisoners were worthy of interrogation from an intel perspective but were still being interrogated. That whole episode led to rewriting the Army doctrine about detention center management and interrogation.

"The 519th was supposed to be conducting interrogations in accordance with the approved U.S. central command procedures. The interrogators were all trained and certified prior to going into the interrogation booth with the detainees. From my perspective, the primary issue with Abu Ghraib, was a leadership failure within the military police and the joint interrogation and debriefing center. The military police abused the detainees as evidenced by the widely circulated photos. The joint interrogation and debriefing center leadership failed to set and maintain appropriate control and supervision of detainees under interrogation. The United States has a humane and thoughtful approach to interrogations. Food, water, religious and sanitary requirements are met multiple times daily and medical treatment is readily available throughout the process. In 2003, Abu Ghraib was the exception. The immediate leaders weren't doing the things they were supposed to be doing. Leadership failures result in mission failures. I'd like to put that on a bumper sticker. That's what we had at Abu Ghraib; mission failure with the custody of the detainees, maintaining good order and discipline. The United States Army failed at Abu Ghraib."

20. "That" Disk

Edwards added: "One thing that sometimes gets lost on units in these environments is discipline, standards and accountability. It starts with the battalion commander, then the command sergeant major and then the two majors in the battalion are working in unity to meet the commander's intent and how the unit should function. They are all bought into the same vision—discipline, standards and accountability. Filter those values and mindset through the ranks and everything should run smoothly."

Captain Romeo Qureishi recalled failures at operational level: "I'll never forget when we got to Abu Ghraib. We were told we had to wear our uniform, our flak vest and salute at all times. Some of the leaders were wondering, 'Why is LTC Walters making us do this?' There's a reason for everything and he knew he had to instill that discipline with all of us that the others did not have. These were standards that were sorely lacking among most of the units that we saw in Abu Ghraib."

Edwards added: "The rule was, if you were walking outside of a hard stand, concrete building, you had to wear your protective equipment. Furthermore, once the sun went down you limited your movements and you had to be careful." Unfortunately, as Major Edwards explained, the flak vest didn't give full coverage: "One of our kids from the administration shop was walking to the bathroom and we got hit with mortars. He got some shrapnel in his behind or his fourth point of contact as we say in the Army. He was taken care of on the base by a medic and I believe he was awarded the Purple Heart because he was hit by shrapnel from an enemy mortar."

Qureishi continued: "People were coming in and out and weren't being checked. It seemed like total chaos and everything was out of control. A lot of the people were workers from Fallujah and you know the reputation which came with that place. Also, a lot of the time, many military personnel were wearing civilian clothes and you didn't know unless they had light skin if they were in the military or they were an Iraqi working there. It was really disorganized."

Walters added: "When you had incoming, typically you would hear an explosion, which was the point of a mortar being launched and then the next sound you would hear would be the sound of it impacting and as soldiers, we were trained on hearing the boom to get down. The military police had a loud horn in case a detainee escaped, which let everyone know in Abu Ghraib that a detainee was loose. That's why I was concerned about everyone being in uniform. I didn't want one of my guys in the security towers, when they heard that horn and saw someone running across the compound with an M-16 not wearing a uniform, to then shoot them and later find out it was a U.S. soldier as opposed to an escaped detainee."

Another shift in behavioral patterns which needed addressing came in the form of graffiti in the latrines. Walters continued: "We didn't know exactly who was doing it. It could have been a soldier or a contractor, but it didn't point towards an Iraqi because it was in colloquial English. It was a U.S. person who was doing it and in fact, probably more than one. There was graffiti of a sexual nature in the bathroom, which was just totally unprofessional. Everybody had to use these facilities on a daily basis, so we started painting over the graffiti with black paint and said to the soldiers in the unit, 'We're not having graffiti in these porta-Johns.' It didn't stop everyone, but it wouldn't last long because we would spray paint over it.

Edwards added: "We walked into an environment where soldiers had peace signs on their helmets and cut off shirt sleeves. We were a disciplined combat unit and when we rolled into something like that, it was shocking. Our immediate response was to establish discipline and standards, but we knew that we had a high hill to climb. Not for us, but for setting standards for the forward operating base. We had an esprit de corps in the battalion. I'm a fan of esprit de corps and not morale. I don't believe in morale because it's a daily thing. Esprit de corps is a long-term thing, having that mutual pride and loyalty amongst the unit. If someone was more focused on their morale, it meant they were focused on themselves. If they were concerned about the esprit de corps, it meant they were concerned about the unit. That stuff I would soapbox on and I believe we had that in the 165th. Other units at Abu Ghraib unfortunately didn't."

Walters clarified: "Just to elaborate, the military police battalion commander was a really nice gentleman. I can't remember his civilian job, but he was a super smart individual. However, when it came to leadership and military leadership in particular, he did not meet the stereotype of a military leader, being aggressive and determined to accomplish whatever task is at hand. He did not meet that stereotype at all. He didn't spend a lot of time with his soldiers, and I never saw him do battlefield circulation. He would come and get their update brief and he would go back to his little office and not come back out until the next day. When you have that sort of absentee style of leadership, problems start to develop, because somebody's going to fill that vacuum and if it's not the right person with the right characteristics and the right motivations, you can really have problems."

◆◆◆

Jump onto any search engine on the internet, type in 'Abu Ghraib' and you are most likely to get hit with a tirade of vile photos of detainee abuse. Walters explained the moment he came into contact with those photos: "One morning I'm walking around doing a perimeter check as part of battlefield circulation, ensuring my soldiers were doing the right thing up in the towers in their security positions. We had a chief warrant officer assigned to Abu Ghraib from the criminal investigation division, who was basically a military police officer that did higher level of crime investigations. He came up to me and said, 'Excuse me sir. I have this disk which has some photos on it. Do you want to look at it, because it has what I consider detainee abuse?' The minute you hear the words detainee abuse, that's an immediate red light and you stop whatever you are doing. You investigate, hold people accountable and ensure the detainees are safe and being treated appropriately. That's ingrained in us growing up in the military. I said, 'Chief. Where did you get this?' and he replied, 'Somebody slid it under my door last night.' I said, 'Okay. Has anybody seen this?' He said, 'No. I brought this straight to you.' I then said, 'Why did you bring it to me?' 'Because you're a battalion commander, so I figured you'd know the right thing to do with it.'

"I said, 'Okay. This is what I want you to do with it. I want you to take this disk straight to our brigade commander (a colonel who had a small office there on the compound) and be prepared to give him your recommendation on how the investigation should proceed. Your experience will help with that.' He said, 'I understand sir. Do you want to see what's on it?' I said, 'None of my soldiers have anything to do with the detainees. We don't hold them, guard them or interrogate them. I don't know who's on there, but I know it's not 165th soldiers. We are in charge of security.' He replied, 'Roger that,' then moved out promptly to brief the colonel.

"Sure enough, once that criminal investigation division officer went in and showed the colonel the disk, he immediately began an investigation. It didn't hit the press until much later, but an Army Regulation 15–6 investigation, led by a Major General commenced immediately. This type of investigation focused on the officers believed to have been

171

involved with the incident in some form, with the intention of specifically establishing if any regulations or standards had been violated. The 15–6 report did that initial investigation and went into great detail about all the players that were involved.

"When our colonel saw the disk, he concurred with the criminal investigation division and contacted the Combined Joint Task Force 7 commander. As expected, a full investigation commenced and everybody that had any knowledge of the photos or the detainee abuse were duly questioned.

"By early 2004, we received word that we were going to be replaced in Abu Ghraib by another battalion. The investigation was still ongoing, had sort of died down, but still hadn't hit the press at this point. When we left Abu Ghraib in March and were driving down Main Supply Route, Tampa towards the Kuwaiti border, I got a call from the provost marshal, who was the senior military police officer in Kuwait. He says, 'Hey Bob. How you doing?' I was a little bit apprehensive because this guy was a colonel and I was a lieutenant colonel, so one grade lower and he's called me by my first name, and I've never met this guy before. He came across a little too friendly. He said, 'Can you come by and see me today?' I said, 'Where are you at Sir?' He replied, 'I'm at my headquarters here in Camp Doha, Kuwait.' I said, 'I'm in a 130-vehicle convoy in Iraq right now, but I should be able to get there tomorrow and I'll come see you right away.' He said, 'That would be great, please come and see me first thing.' I said, 'Okay sir,' and hung up.

"I turned to my sergeant major and wanted to know which of our long-range surveillance guys we sent to Camp Doha, Kuwait, because I was sure they'd done something to get in trouble, which is why I thought the provost marshal wanted to speak to me. However, that wasn't the case. When we got to Camp Doha, the battalion was washing vehicles, accounting for equipment, doing all those logistical things you have to do to redeploy a unit. I went to see this colonel and as soon as I walked in, I was introduced to about six lawyers and they read me my rights. This was the 15–6 investigation."

On February 14, 2004, which was coincidentally Walters' twenty-third wedding anniversary, a panel of officers interviewed him: "We were all questioned by the team about what happened and when. To my knowledge I was the only member of the 165th to be interviewed. I think a large reason for that is because when I described the 165th at Abu Ghraib to the investigators, they realized that they were not involved with detainee handling or interrogation. I have to tell you, it was a hostile interview to say the least. It was like they were the sharks and I was flounder flopping around there, about to be consumed.

"They started questioning me in a hostile manner about everything to do with the detainee abuse and everything that happened in Abu Ghraib at the time. My opinion was that they were convinced I was personally abusing the detainees and taking pictures with my cell phone. That was obviously not the case and when I explained everything to them, they said, 'Thank you. We'll be in touch,' but they never did get back in touch."

Major Mickie Williams added: "I would come into Abu Ghraib every other day just to sync up with our brigade commander. I distinctly remember the day he was first advised of the pictures. I arrived and he pushed me out of his office, telling me, 'I'm dealing with something.' It was something at that point he didn't want me to be involved with and said he just wanted a separation of what he wanted me to focus on."

Walters continued: "We got back to Germany in March 2004 and one of my counter intelligence officers stuck his head in my door and said, 'We found some classified information on the internet.' I said, 'Okay. Don't download it. Get the IP address and notify the brigade of that compromise.' He said, 'Your name is on it.' I thought, 'Oh shit!' Somehow, someone got their hands on the 15–6 report and put it on the internet, while it was still classified. That carried a lot of empirical data from the event and gave the media a field day."

Spring 2004, *The New Yorker* and *60 Minutes* released the photos, and the story broke across the world. Those photos really put Abu Ghraib on an unfortunate map and the detail was damning to say the least. Thankfully, Walters' integrity as a person and commander shone through as Page 49 of the 15–6 Report explained:

Throughout the investigation, we observed many individual soldiers and some subordinate units under the 800th MP Brigade that overcame significant obstacles, persevered in extremely poor conditions, and upheld the Army Values. We discovered numerous examples of soldiers and sailors taking the initiative in the absence of leadership and accomplishing their assigned tasks.

The 165th MI Battalion excelled in providing perimeter security and force protection at Abu Ghraib (BCCF). LTC Robert P. Walters, Jr., demanded standards be enforced and worked endlessly to improve discipline throughout the FOB (forward operating base).

Finishing on a light-hearted note, Walters recalled an anecdote: "Immediately after we handed in the disk, I told the company commander, 'There's going to be an investigation here, so if any of your soldiers have anything that they should not have, like pornographic material, they need to get rid of it, because people are going to be looking for it.'

"We had a bonfire and all these young soldiers who had pornographic material mailed to them by their loved ones back home were throwing these pictures into the fire and standing there literally crying as they watched pictures of their topless girlfriend go up in smoke."

For now, the time had come for the battalion to wave goodbye to the Middle East, head back to European soil and prepare for a change of command and new deployment.

21

Home Time

"Other things may change us, but we start and end with the family."—Anthony Brandt

After over a month in Kuwait, the 165th Military Intelligence Battalion eventually boarded their ride home. Major Edwards recalled: "We finally get on our aircraft at Camp Wolf, however we got stuck in Crete, Greece, sitting on the tarmac for about nine hours, because there was some issue with flying over airspace. Almost the entire battalion was on this plane, around three hundred people, so they opened up all the doors so we could get air into the craft. In the meantime, the families at home thought we were going to be at Rhein-Main airbase in Germany at a certain time. Dana went back and forward to the airfield three or four times during that day."

Dana added: "At first, we went to the airport awaiting the homecoming and then we found out the plane was delayed in Crete, so we went home and waited. As you can imagine, it wasn't easy with a toddler, trying to keep Elise entertained and telling Madeline after she's asked, 'When's daddy coming home?' and answering, 'I think it's going to happen soon,' but you can't say with certainty, because actually you don't know what's going on. I tried to be upbeat and positive for them, but it was emotionally exhausting not knowing the timing and what was going on.

"After several hours we went back to the unit. By this stage it was very late and Elise was tired as it was her bedtime. The area we were waiting in was small and the energy in the room was chaotic, because everyone's emotions were so high because they were seeing their loved ones after such a long and volatile time. The anticipation was crazy. Everyone was physically anxious to physically see their soldier."

Edwards recalled the moment he reconnected with his family after an extensive combat deployment in Iraq: "With that long layover in Crete, we had spent almost 24 hours making our way back to Germany and by the time we landed at Rhein-Main airbase it was late at night. We then bussed back to the battalion headquarters in Darmstadt, which was about thirty minutes away from the airport."

Dana added: "It was dark when we saw the bus come around the corner and we waited for the soldiers to make their way off. I remember scanning the crowd and finally seeing Bill. It didn't seem real and it took a matter of time to sink in. The girls were tired, but very excited. It was very emotional and felt like a dream."

Edwards continued: "Dana and the girls were waiting in the parking lot with all the families and despite it being very dark, we found each other and gave each other some big hugs. It was surreal, exciting and amazing to see them, but it was also awkward as we had been apart for so long. We then loaded up our car and I drove us home to our apartment in Langen which was near Frankfurt airport. I hadn't driven in a while and didn't remember where we lived. I kept asking, 'Which exit do I take?' while the girls fell asleep in the car."

Walters gave his take on the homecoming: "I remember standing at the doorway of the plane when we were on the runway in Crete and looking out over the Mediterranean. It was beautiful. The feeling that I had at that point was that I was very happy that I had all of these soldiers safely out of the warzone. To be able to stand there and look out over the Mediterranean Sea and feel the breeze blowing, that was a very comforting feeling. I don't recall the number of hours we were on the tarmac, but it didn't matter, because we were not getting shot at, we were not getting mortared, and we did not have to write any letters home to parents of fallen soldiers or anything of that nature. I was happy.

"When we arrived in Germany, that's where we transferred our weapons. One of the things you did not want to have was soldiers, family members and weapons all together at the same time. We handed in the weapons at Rhein-Main where everything was under military control and there were no civilians involved. After that was done, we got on the buses, and as Bill said, it was about thirty minutes until we arrived to meet with our families in Darmstadt.

"The rear detachment was phenomenal in all this. There was a young lieutenant who was a superb officer and an incredible contrast to his predecessor. When we deployed from Germany, we still had a platoon of about thirty soldiers down in Kosovo. They were going to be there for about three months before they deployed back to Germany. I had a lieutenant who I wasn't very impressed with, simply because she was not a very effective leader. I made the decision that she was probably my most expendable officer and I put her in charge of rear detachment, which was a horrible decision on my part, because the rear detachment is the interface with the community, family members of the deployed soldiers and unit. The rear detachment is also the element that organizes transportation to get replacement personnel into theater. I entrusted her with a position of responsibility that was well beyond her capabilities. This officer did a horrible job, and I should have known that was going to be the case. Instead of being focused on the mission in Kuwait and then Iraq, I was looking backwards to Germany, trying to figure things out that should have been done by that rear detachment commander.

"So, when the platoon that was in Kosovo redeployed to Germany, I made that platoon leader the rear detachment commander. A superb soldier who was a very talented graduate from West Point. He did really well for us and we were lucky to have him.

"Back to our arrival in Germany in March 2004, the rear detachment commander arranged, managed and lead the rear detachment through most of our deployment. I told him my concerns before we left from Kuwait that I didn't want family members and weapons in the same place at the same time, because if you lose a weapon, you're not just dealing with soldiers in a military environment, now you've got civilians and everything else gets very complicated. He set up a way for us when we got off the plane to turn our weapons in. This was not a sophisticated process. You basically put them into the back of a truck and have a non-commissioned officer from rear detachment giving accountability for the items.

"Then we drove to Darmstadt to our barracks area. I recall my daughter Daytona had taken a bed sheet and painted the 165th logo on it and had also painted 'welcome home' on it. The rear detachment family readiness group did an amazing job prior to us getting off the bus in Darmstadt. All the families had gone through the barracks of the soldiers that were deployed and decorated their doors with gift wrapping paper and put little notes like, 'We love you,' 'So happy you are back,' on them. They also gave little bags for the soldiers coming back that were living in the barracks, with toiletries, snacks and that type of stuff and left them in the rooms. Again, that rear detachment commander was the guy that supported all this, along with the family readiness group members.

"So, when we got off the bus it was nothing but hugs and tears and the local media was there. It was a very joyful event coming home and seeing all those family members and the rear detachment. We also got to see some of these were guys who had been deployed and came back early, so again, a lot of hugs a lot of cheers. It was a very positive reception and was just what was needed after spending months in a place like Abu Ghraib."

The relief of reuniting with family after such an intense and dangerous deployment was certainly evident. However, readjustment to normality did not happen at the flick of a switch, if at all.

22

Child's Perspective

"Nearly two million children in the United States have at least one parent in the military."—Department of Defense, 2012

When a parent is deployed into a combat environment, the uncertainty of the individual's return due to the dangerous circumstances plays heavily on the family and loved ones left behind. The parent back at base provide as much stability as possible for the children from schooling, military and family perspectives.

For the children, comprehending the depth to their multiple ecologies isn't always the easiest of rides. Getting to grips with their father's vocation was the initial challenge. Walters' daughter, Daytona, explained. "My first memories of understanding about what my father did for work was Desert Shield/Desert Storm. I was very young but understood Papa might not come home.

"Hindsight being what it is, when it came to Operation Iraqi Freedom, I think I was angry was because I hated there was a reason that made it okay for Papa to leave again and not knowing if he'd come back. I felt left behind. I struggled with the amount of fear I felt and lack of control over any of what was happening. Once, when I was ten years old, I wrote the President a letter on my Winnie the Pooh stationery, letting him know my dad deserved a break.

"During Operation Iraqi Freedom 1, I didn't write him as often as he wrote me and I was nervous to send him presents for his birthday or holidays. I was afraid he'd die and a stranger would see them or that he'd have to discard them if they took up too much room. I was angry he was gone and was afraid of him not coming home. I regret not writing him more during that deployment. It was a tough year."

Sister Martina added: "My earliest memories of military life are from Fort Huachuca, Arizona. This was late 1980s and not during war time. The extent of my knowledge to my dad being in the Army was that he wore a uniform and kept us safe.

"Communication varied. My dad is very thoughtful and was more diligent in writing to me, and everyone important to him, than I was to him. If things were more stable, we'd share updates of school, work, friends, etc. The nature of the deployment, would depend on how we would communicate. If he was calling from a satellite phone in the middle of nowhere with spotty connection, I just made sure I said, "Be safe and I love you."

"The first combat deployment was Desert Shield/Storm in 1990. I was still quite young. I remember being afraid he would be killed but I also knew if the President said our Army needed to be somewhere, of course he would go. As the deployments continued, I spent less time worrying about him being killed though I knew it was a risk."

Elise recalled: "I did not really understand my dad's work for years, but when I was eight or nine years old, he was in command and set to deploy again and by then I had a better understanding of his work. That's when I realized, every time I'd say goodbye to him, that could be the last time I saw him. The burden of having that thought in the back of my mind took a toll on me as a young child. My classmate's father had been killed in Iraq and I realized, by this age that could happen to my father also."

The most poignant recollection comes from Elise's sister, Madeline: "I always knew my dad was in the Army, however before 9/11 that didn't really mean that much. To me, at that age, it was just another job that a parent could have. I think I was just too young to understand, it wasn't even a case of ignorance is bliss. The first time he was deployed, I knew he was in danger, but the second time was a little bit harder because I knew he was in danger and there started to be a lot of negative emotions towards the Iraq war from the general public. Having a parent in the military is very intense. You swing between intense pride and intense fear. On top of that, everyone in the world has an opinion on your parent's career. When everything is so personal, you don't want to have or hear anyone's opinion on the war or politics. You just want to be proud of your dad and afraid for him. But that can be isolating if you don't live around other military families because you don't know how people will respond when the war is brought up. It is hard to experience such intense emotions and feel somewhat alone.

22. Child's Perspective

"Even after 9/11, I didn't really consider the life-threatening implications of my dad's job until the day he deployed for Iraq, when I was nine. For whatever reason, he left and came back two or three times. For two or three days in a row, I said an emotional goodbye to my father, while for the first time considering I would never see him again. On either the third or fourth day, I was at the playground near our apartment complex when he was leaving, and I chose not to go home to say goodbye. I didn't think he would actually leave, but of course, this time he did. I had to sleep with my mom for two weeks often crying because I thought 'What if something happens to him and you didn't get the chance to say goodbye?' This experience was the first time I considered what my dad being in the military really meant."

To many, travelling to pastures new and experiencing different cultures, food and languages can be a very exciting prospect, but minus the uncertainty of when the next move might happen is perhaps not as appealing. Martina explained: "I did most of fifth grade, sixth and all but two months of seventh grades at the same school. We lived off-post in a rural community, everyone knew each other and no one ever left. The last two months of seventh grade we moved to Maryland. The school was much larger and I experienced some serious culture shock. The East Coast pace was quite an adjustment. I remember coming home from school crying, telling my mom I didn't know why I was crying but that I wanted to go back. I didn't like being the new girl.

"We ended up moving several more times over the next few years, resulting in my attending three high schools. That was hard but, thankfully, my dad was able to adjust his assignments so I could complete my last year of high school in the same place I attended my junior year. I am very grateful for that. When my friends would talk about family traditions with extended family or going to the same event every year, I wondered what that was like. My feelings on the subject were a combination of envy and boredom, though I am keenly aware that most families take their geography for granted."

Daytona experienced more heated emotions: "I spent more time angry at other families not seeming to understand or care what was happening in the rest of the world. I didn't think they 'got it,' if that makes sense? I felt like we were outsiders, especially when we went to off-post schools. I wanted to stop moving, but not to be like other people, I was always proud of our family. I just wanted to stop saying goodbye and uprooting. Moving is tiring."

Inside Abu Ghraib

Madeline found loneliness to be a testing factor: "When we lived in communities that did not have many military families, the Iraq War had not started. Once it started, we often lived and socialized with a lot of other military families, so I wasn't around a lot of people who had a different experience than myself. The only time I really felt being in a military family was different was towards the end of middle school and the beginning of high school. A lot of people had had the same friends since kindergarten and I had a hard time 'breaking in.' I did wonder what it was like to have a life-long friend at the time. It took me until my junior year of high school to make friends I still keep in touch with now.

"At the time it was a little isolating moving to a community where people had never moved for a long time and I felt I would never truly be a part of. Actually, in some ways that were true, there are lots of weddings for people at my high school I am not invited to and a large contingent of people that still hang out, which I have not spoken to in years. I could never have that because I simply wasn't there from the beginning."

Dana Edwards added: "The constant moving was tough for Madeline and Elise. In addition to moving all the contents of the house, the girls went to nine different schools in twelve years. Stop and think about that for a moment."

Looking from another perspective, Madeline reminisced about the positive aspects of the nomadic nature of being the daughter of a military officer: "Moving a lot had its ups and downs. The good part was we got to live in a lot of different places. We lived in Germany and also eventually settled in Colorado which I loved and chose to stay there for my undergraduate degree. We took a lot of fun trips we would not have been otherwise been able to take. For instance, we went skiing in Arabba, Italy with a few other families. It was so fun because we would ski all day then hang out in the hotel at night. Our parents could drink wine and we would play. The bar in the hotel sometimes played 'kid music' so all the kids would dance. There was a restaurant that served the best hot chocolate in the world, it was so thick. My sister, Elise told them her favorite animal was an elephant so the whole time we were there they gave her the hot chocolate in an elephant mug and then at the end of the trip they let her keep it. This was the type of place we would have never seen if my dad hadn't been in the Army. Even living in Heidelberg, Germany was a really neat experience for me. When I was in 6th grade my parents would let me take the Stassenbahn (tram) to the Hauptstrasse with my friends and walk around. It felt so cool and independent at the time. In the U.S., since you have to drive everywhere, I could have never had that much independence at that young of an age.

"Another place that was really memorable for me as a child was visiting Rome. I loved the history and would soak up information on every tour we took, I particularly remember learning the story of Romulus and Remus and the founding of Rome. We would drive to Vicenza, Italy and leave our car on an Army post there. Then from there, we would take the train to travel to different places like Pisa, Rome, and Florence. I mostly remember how kind people were at all of the little restaurants we ate at and how beautiful the architecture was. Overall, by the time I was thirteen I had a great appreciation for art, history, food, and language. This absolutely shaped my interests to this day. I am so happy I got to see so many places at a formative age and I know we could not have done this without the Army.

"And when my dad got back, the next two years were really fun. We did a lot of traveling as a family and got to have a lot of cultural experiences and as a result I still love to travel to this day. It was also fun at times to be a part of the military community. In Heidelberg, for instance, all my friends' parents were also in the military and it really felt like a community. We went to school together, played soccer together, and everyone felt pretty equal like we were all on the same page. The sense of community could be very strong, it wasn't at every single place we lived, but it could be."

Nancy explained her perspective as a mother: "Every deployment brought its own set of circumstances and needs to be met for my children. For me, I wanted to respect whatever age they were for each deployment and meet their age appropriate needs. As a military family there is very little you have control of, and in a deployment, it is exacerbated. I wanted them to know their father loved them and was doing what he had to do. But that means little to children when the parent is just not there, regardless of why. Most spouses have to be both parents during a deployment.

"However, we would always try to put a positive spin on the adventure ahead for a new deployment. We'd normally donate items before the movers came and try to streamline what was possible, with the motivation being the girls would get to pick out new bedding and new bedroom décor at our next place. When they were little that worked well because they were happy as long as we were together. In middle school and high school that was not the case.

"Although moving is a challenge it was always a great adventure. Every place we lived or got to visit taught us that everywhere people are doing a lot of the same things. Falling in love, getting married, having children, trying to raise them and pay bills. No one place is the center of the universe, just another dot on a very huge map.

"We got to experience and learn about different traditions, and taste all kinds of differently prepared foods, drink great wine in Italy and flip pancakes in England. We met folks who are still great friends to this day, that we would have never met. We have attended great formal balls and competed in unit organization days. Our inside jokes are ours forever. And even though we never lived anywhere very long, as a family our roots are very deep and forged together, not in one place but in each other. It is an awesome feeling to see the flag, knowing the cost of keeping it flying."

Daytona added: "We call ourselves the Core 4. That name comes from how often we were each other's only friends whenever we moved. It comes from the inside jokes, comedy of errors that accompanied moves, family trips and navigating life together. Because of our life, we don't take much for granted, we appreciate a good single malt, and love fiercely. If I were to list all the positive memories, it'd be enough to fill several books. I wouldn't trade any part of our life for another. We honor the cross and the flag and hope what our family went through can help support the next generation of those called to serve."

◈◈◈

Being told to keep your chin up and Charlie Mike is easier said than done. Operation Iraqi Freedom 1 came with unexpected emotional ramifications. Madeline recalled: "We moved to Germany, then my dad left. It happened very quickly and I became a lot more sensitive while he was gone. Out of nowhere I would cry in movies and be unable to finish them (productions like *The Fox and the Hound* or *The Hunchback of Notre Dame*). I also had a moment in Cologne, Germany when we were going to go to the top of a church where I became afraid of heights and was too scared to go up it."

Elise, who had also experienced an episode of panic at the Christmas market, added: "Another similar occasion was when my sister was in fourth grade and I was three or four at the time and my mom took me to her fourth grade class Halloween party. Someone's mask scared me and I screamed and cried for hours for my dad, but I didn't know where he was. That was really hard on my mom because she didn't know what to tell me."

Dana continued: "You try to do normal things like go to the park, the library, take a walk, drive to Cologne, visit the cathedral, go to the Christmas market. We had a daily schedule and didn't think about Bill. I'd also say, 'Daddy is fine and he's going to come home soon,' but without a timeframe, it was hard. You don't think you are stressed out, but it suddenly comes out in mysterious ways and that trip it happened with both of them."

Madeline continued: "When he was on deployment in Iraq, we were much more on edge and wouldn't sit and talk about the danger he was in, which probably wouldn't have helped anybody anyway. We sucked it up and tried to do family stuff, but I do think we were much more sensitive and when small things happened, we were much more apt to snap. When my sister was screaming, 'I want my dad,' and I had that panic attack, which was totally out of character for me, because I'd never had one before and wasn't afraid of heights either, it was because we were really shaken. I was lucky that year dad was gone that I had a very good teacher, so I was fine at school, but outside of school, when anything happened, it was far more disastrous, whether you are acknowledging it or not.

"I also had a very hard time sleeping the year my dad was gone but didn't really link the two things at the time. My mom used to come in and check on me every night before she went to bed and I would pretend to be asleep. One night I didn't pretend to be asleep and she was really shocked to find me awake, so I just pretended to be asleep the rest of the nights when she came in. The second time he was deployed I was in high school, I just told myself 'It wasn't a big deal, Iraq had gotten safer,' or 'It wouldn't be as dangerous as the first time,' or 'We'll talk to him more so it will be easier.' In the end, I actually think this time was much harder for me because I understood more. I could also see the toll this deployment took on my mom, which was difficult to witness."

At the age of three, after dropping her father off at the airport for deployment with sister Madeline and mother Dana, Elise couldn't comprehend why her father hadn't returned home. With a limited memory available to her at that age, she pieced together a rationale and assumed her father was lost at the airport and would be home soon: "I was very young when my dad was doing what he was doing in Iraq and really didn't know what was going on. It was a very confusing time for me.

My mom was constantly trying to keep me distracted and sugar-coating things. Obviously, you don't want to explain to a three year old that your father is in Iraq. I had this confusion of where he was.

"But then every time I received news that my dad would be deployed, I felt heartbroken. He's my dad and he was the one who put band-aids on my scrapes, carried me on his shoulders, cracked jokes with me and took all of my problems like they were his own. He helped me solve any situation and made me feel secure and I felt the loss of that when he was gone. I felt like my dad's welfare was a constant state of confusion and anxiety."

It's well documented that the quality of relationships between children and the parent deployed will experience an element of stress. Madeline explained from her perspective: "When he was away the quality of the relationship was lower, but I never held that against him. Especially the first deployment, we spoke maybe one or two times and when we did, it was nice to hear his voice but a little awkward because we were very rushed and had nothing to talk about.

"During his second deployment, we talked weekly or monthly, which was better, but you cannot replace being together, with anyone. I knew he was sad to miss things, and we were sad to have him miss things, but it really didn't affect our relationship in the long run. During those conversations we mostly talked about me and what was going on at school, how were sports, etc. Or we talked about movies. Sometimes my dad would watch pirated movies that were out in the U.S. that people sold in Iraq. If we saw the same movie we would discuss that, but it was mostly surface-level conversation. I don't think the funny conversations or really exchanging of stories happened until he was home. I think while he was gone, it's not that it was tense but we were just working so hard to keep everything as normal as possible and he didn't share with us any details of what was going on there. Also, since Elise and I were kids at the time, I don't know what he could have even told us anyway.

"It always took some time for things to get back to normal when he returned. From the first deployment, I remember when he got back, he was always cold. I also remember we had made great friends with all of the people in our building and he had completely missed that, so I think it was a bit awkward for him.

"During the second deployment, I aged a lot while he was gone, and I got my driver's license. I think it was a little hard for him to adjust to how much freedom I had. I didn't have a very strict curfew because I was usually pretty good and my mom knew my friends. I remember one time I was hanging out with a group of friends at my friend Zach's house and got home very late. We weren't doing anything nefarious, but I remember my dad telling me I wasn't allowed to stay out that late now that he was home. It took us a little bit for him to adjust to how much I had grown in the year he was gone, but overall it wasn't a terrible transition."

All transitions within the military come with adjustments and Operation Iraqi Freedom 1 certainly left its mark on the families. Getting back to conventional life was an unknown quantity.

23

Adjustment

"To study the abnormal is the best way of understanding the normal."—William James

Deployment has been associated with poorer mental and physical health in families, higher divorce rates, lack of family cohesion, behavioral problems with children, increased usage of alcohol and drugs, and on occasions even suicide. Nancy discussed her own experience as a military wife: "The flow of life and living endured, continued with the family back home and the deployed soldier. I believe the memories of what life was like before a deployment carried many through, but on the other side it was no longer a true reality that could be obtained in a few days, weeks or months.

"The unrealistic expectation of 'normal' was the greatest destructor to families. No family can go back or return to what it was before a deployment. Due to multiple war fronts and continuous deployments, the Army invested heavily into everything it could to help families, soldiers and marriages, for pre-deployment, during deployment and post deployment. They re-defined normal as the 'new normal.'

"The reaction to this 'new normal' term amongst military families varied. It went from bitterness, because they felt the Army was trying to justify separation, to relief, that the spouse did not feel the burden of getting their family back to what it was before the deployment, simply because many spouses felt that was their job to do. That, however, did not change how children dealt with and reacted before, during and after. And it varied depending on the age of the child.

Nancy continued: "I have friends whose children went off the rails and were never able to get back, and also know spouses and marriages that did the same. There should never be judgment over them. Waiting for someone you love, knowing they might not come back, standing at gravesides, attending memorials, waiting for any information or message that your loved one is alright, that the unit is alright day in and day out for months on end—no child, regardless of their age signed up for that. It changes everyone. Tragically, good marriages failed just because they had been separated by long deployments one too many times. However, I do know many who were and are resilient beyond comprehension, home front warriors that endured and some who are enduring today."

Knowing LTC Walters' routine and what he might encounter on deployment, was the pressure of holding the fort for the family as tough as she had imagined? "Tougher. As Charles Dickens said in his book *A Tale of Two Cities,* Operation Iraqi Freedom 1 was and still remains 'the best of times and the worst of times.' However, I must really emphasize our stories are not more or less unique than any other military family. There are thousands more out there."

Edwards reflected on returning home after Operation Iraqi Freedom 1 deployment: "We had thirty days of leave when we got back from Abu Ghraib and we were supposed to be working again on all the reintegration and reconstitution. At the time, the Army had not worked out the complexities of reintegration with the family. That got better over the years, but those days, we were the test case of how this was all going to work out.

"With Operation Iraqi Freedom 1, we didn't know how long the conflict was going to go on for and at the time there wasn't an official rest and recuperation program. However, they realized, 'We're going to have to do this because we are keeping soldiers in combat zones for fourteen months.' What's a bit different from our deployment in Iraq compared to say WW1 and WW2, is that, in those conflicts soldiers were rotated into the combat zone and then they rotated back off the front line and given rest and recuperation. But in this conflict, we were in the combat zone 24/7.

"When driving from Baghdad to Balad for supplies, I'd constantly be looking for piles of trash or rocks, that might indicate there was an explosive device on the road. As you can imagine, our stress levels were very high. So, when I got home, all I wanted to do was just be normal. One of the things I remember vividly was transitioning from desert uniforms to woodland. To me, that was not only a physical, but a mental transition to remind us that we were not in Iraq anymore. We went back to what was called the battle dress uniform, which was a green camouflage uniform and had different boots. It was like a weight being lifted off my shoulders wearing that uniform. The other thing was, Germany felt really calm to me. When we were in Darmstadt, we had a really nice forest outside of our battalion headquarters and in the morning I would run in that forest, then I'd shower at the battalion headquarters and it just felt like a normal routine. My car was in the parking lot and all those kind of normal things reminded me that I wasn't downrange.

"Back home though, it took a bit longer to adjust. It wasn't a Hollywood style return to home. My girls never asked me about what I was doing in Abu Ghraib and maybe they could sense that was a sensitive area to approach. When I did talk, I tried to focus on the funny things that happened downrange instead of the nightmares. I wanted to get home, sleep in my bed, drive our car, go to a coffee shop, go to a bakery, take the family on a vacation."

Dana gave her recollections from a mother and wife's perspective: "Elise stuck to me like glue, very wary of the person that disappeared from her life, whereas Madeline was older, but the adjustment at that time was cloudy for her. Me personally, I was doing my best to just absorb it all."

"I would say parenting during deployments is very difficult in that the sole decisions and responsibilities rest on your shoulders. Fortunately, because of the numerous moves we had been through, sixteen in total, the girls and I are very close. When you move to a new city and the only people you know are your family, you rely on them heavily and that creates a strong bond.

"Madeline and Elise were thankfully healthy, well-adjusted and made friends easily. As far as our marriage, I don't know if absence truly makes the heart grow fonder, but it certainly makes you appreciate the little things. The first time I awoke when Bill got home and there was coffee already made, I cried. I was just so happy to share a coffee at my home with my husband. Other little things like mowing the lawn, buying tires for the car, getting the oil changed, driving to riding lessons and doing everyday tasks to divide I was so grateful for the help.

"When we got to the apartment, the place we had been living for the last year, I kind of had to introduce Bill to our home. He didn't know where the dishes, towels or cups would go or where we put the mail. But that didn't matter. There was always a bit of humor when Bill would say, 'This is my house and I don't know where anything is!' From my point of view, I don't think we ever talked about Operation Iraqi Freedom 1. The gratitude of him actually coming home was immense and I didn't want to upset him by asking questions like, 'Did you witness anyone dying?' I didn't know what to ask and there were no classes or any guidelines to reintegration for your spouse on return from combat deployment. Things like, these are questions you should avoid, or maybe this is a good way for you to approach if you are curious or to check if they are mentally healthy. Nothing. My thoughts were, if there's an issue he wants to talk about, I'll let him open up. I didn't want to trigger anything.

"Bill was different after this deployment. I am not sure it was obviously noticeable, but I knew. We would go and have lunch with the girls, and he was taken aback a bit, by how the world just goes on, while others are sacrificing their lives. It was so incredible to him that people would be so concerned about mundane things that no longer seemed significant to him."

Edwards added: "I think the transition back to normal society is something every soldier goes through. For me, normality was an odd transition based on our experiences in Iraq and certain things took a long time adjust. I also think I was anxious, very tired and easier to anger over things I might not have taken as seriously before. I guess I felt disdain at the time. Going from the pace we were on to the pace of normal life is simply not normal. It took about half a year to ease back in."

Dana continued: "He started experiencing health issues as well, including the inability to sleep for more than a couple hours, constantly checking to see if the house was secure and a racing heart. Bill was referred to a cardiologist and he was diagnosed with premature ventricular contractions, due to the adrenaline and stress which had changed his heartbeat rhythm. Fortunately, Bill was able to implement lifestyle changes and was able to manage this.

"In 2008, when Bill was a battalion commander, we attended the pre-command at Fort Leavenworth. We were asked to form a motto for how we would like to support the families and soldiers of the unit. I remember our motto was 'Professional, Positive, and Patient.' I reflected on that a lot during that subsequent deployment. I especially appreciated while Bill was in command, the pressure Bob and Nancy must have experienced. I was fortunate for Nancy's support. I was welcomed into the unit and although there was no formal assistance or support, I felt like Nancy was available. She did not put pressure on us and she understood my hands were tied by distance to the unit and my children.

"While Bill was in battalion command years later, there were more formal assistance programs. The Army had a military and family life counselor, assigned to each brigade, who would attend monthly meetings to try and connect with the spouses. The support increased, but the spouses' responsibilities also increased. There was a feeling that we are all in this together, but there was also a feeling that in a leadership role you need to be strong, because you were a face of the unit. Although I felt the pressure, most days I felt strong and happy just to be with my girls.

"Throughout a deployment, you want to make everything feel normal and safe even if you are in a new house or country. We focused on daily activities and celebrating birthdays, Christmas and other holidays, making positive new memories together. However, I felt a certain amount of guilt enjoying beautiful dinners and having fun with Madeline and Elise knowing Bill was in austere conditions. As the sole parent, there was a 'must go on attitude,' which I now see how exhausting it was, although, I did not realize it at the time.

"As spouses, we did talk at unit functions or meetings, but mainly about each other's daily activities. It is as if no one really wanted to address the elephant in the room, the actual stress of what we were dealing with. Of course, if it was a memorial, we were just so sad for the families involved and knew we had to count our blessings. My stress levels were under control, for the most part, I felt. The joy of being a mom and watching my children grow and learn gave me much happiness. However, even to this day when I see a moving truck, I have to take a deep breath and recall how much work is involved being in the military.

"When asked if things got back to normal? No, things never got back to normal. The routine of military lifestyle does not get easier over time, you just know you can manage it because you have done it before and there are a lot of others who have endured deployments and many other hardships.

"Revisiting those feelings, sharing and reflecting on them after all these years has been a difficult process. There was always a bit of the stiff upper lip which was adopted. Whatever needed to be done was done. You needed to be strong and not emotional. For me, talking about this in the book has made me realize, 'Wow. That was really hard and lonesome.' Talking about it now has been more difficult than I remember just going through it."

◆◆◆

23. *Adjustment*

Post-traumatic stress disorder (PTSD) is a well-documented common by-product of wartime deployment. As we embark into the 2020s, Major Edwards reflected on how much of an issue PTSD posed: "It wasn't well known or talked about. After Operation Iraqi Freedom 1, it was a very significant issue that the Army took seriously, as time showed the wounds of PTSD on the force. During the early deployments, not much was known. The effects are not always evident and are sometimes triggered by normal things. For example, I was very sensitive to loud and abrupt noises. Those types of sounds meant danger downrange but were completely harmless in normal society. The sound of a car backfire, or the time my daughter kicked her soccer ball against our metal garage door in Germany."

Walters added: "Same for me, I still react to loud, sharp noises. I'm not sure if that is PTSD or situational awareness and caution."

Walters' daughter, Martina, recalled: "I am not sure our transient lifestyle caused PTSD. Our family has certainly endured some valleys, like everyone. The resiliency that is a product of military life certainly helped us continue moving forward even when it seemed impossible to do so. Some of those events were remarkably traumatic though."

Edwards' daughter, Madeline, added: "I do not believe I have PTSD, but I do believe I think about terrorism more than someone who did not have a father in the military. It subconsciously makes me very nervous in certain situations. For instance, I think I am hyperaware of my surroundings and I'm suspicious of people in situations like being on public transit. It makes me nervous to be in the same subway car with irrational people. I also do not stand too close to the tracks and usually keep my back to a wall. Terrorism was something that was always on my radar with my dad being in the Army. I generally think I am a bit more worried about safety in regard to terrorism than the average person."

Living life in the fast lane can often take its toll on soldiers attempting to adjust to civilian life. Edwards explained: "After Operation Iraqi Freedom 1, a lot of soldiers came back and felt like there were no limits in their life and that they were invincible. They'd been through something and thought, nothing else could be as bad as that. They would drive fast, especially on the autobahns in Germany, where there was no speed limit, but also live equally as fast. Deployment does have its effects. There were ramifications for people who were involved in high intensity situations, and we didn't have a good system to address that."

Walters added: "From my perspective and from what I've seen, people handle stress during deployments in different ways. Some handle it positively, focusing on rigorous physical fitness and others put a lot of energy into communicating with their spouse and children, both of which are very positive. The other thing that helped was focusing on was Army values. I'm talking about loyalty, duty, respect, selfless service, honor, integrity and personal courage. If you have your soldiers focused on that, it helps to keep them away from the negative activities that cause problems.

"Unfortunately, some people find it difficult to focus on positive things and then face other challenges as a result of that. I had an experience when I took over a brigade command a few years later. In one of the battalions, there was a soldier who went out and bought himself a brand-new motorcycle. That Saturday, he went out, was driving too fast, operating beyond his capability and experience level, and unfortunately died. That was really tough on his parents, because he was a single soldier. Up to that point, his parents were relieved that their son had gone through a year plus deployment and was home for a couple of weeks. Then he was dead. That was very sad. The way people cope with adjusting to normal life varies with the individual and sadly, the negative ways have repercussions."

24

Clocking Out

"As we express our gratitude, we must never forget that the highest appreciation is not to utter words, but to live by them."—John F. Kennedy

Returning to Germany was a massive relief to all the soldiers from the 165th, but even while they were catching up on valuable family time, logistically, there were still a few loose ends to tie up. Major Edwards recalled: "The U.S. Army Europe Command was implementing a reconstitution program for all of the redeploying units from theater who had started to rotate back to Germany and the U.S. In Europe specifically, there was a program that we could get our equipment into these reconstitution and maintenance facilities all over Germany and get them fixed and to operational capability. I think we had a forty-five-day window in which they were trying to jam all this equipment through, which was a little bit ambitious, based on what was coming back and the condition that some of the equipment was in.

"We started organizing groups, by company, as equipment was coming into Antwerp then started working the redeployment plan from there to Darmstadt. The soldiers internal to our battalion were on that. Some of the equipment we put on trains back to Darmstadt and some of it we had to drive back which took a couple of days. The plan involved a lot of coordination, but it wasn't hard stuff and we weren't in Iraq any more. We were also aware that the soldiers were back from deployment, and we didn't want to burn them out."

LTC Walters explained: "The battalion still had to operate, even though eighty percent were on block leave. The rear detachment commander ran the show while we were all on leave. Of course, he kept leadership informed, but he and the soldiers kept operations functional until we returned from leave. Then we'd deactivate the rear detachment and it was just regular battalion operations.

"You wanted to reintegrate the personnel with their families and you wanted to reconstitute the property of the battalion that was damaged or destroyed, because they didn't know then when they would be redeploying back to Iraq or Afghanistan again, but they knew it was going to happen at some point in the not too distant future. They had to get that equipment that had been damaged and needed to be fixed and we had to get it up to what we called 10–20 standard, so it was ready for the next deployment. Although, little did we know, at the time of writing this book, seventeen years later we are still there. This has been a long conflict."

Edwards added: "10–20 is the technical term that comes with the manual for technical equipment. There's a Dash 10 manual. So, if I'm a driver of a truck it will tell me to clean the windows, change the wiper fluid, the tire pressure, that sort of thing. Dash 20 is the next level of maintenance, where you would have a true mechanic working off a

Bullet hole from a recent patrol in the Abu Ghraib area of operations (William Edwards' collection).

Dash 20 technical manual. At Abu Ghraib, we had a maintenance section in the battalion, which was in charge of keeping our entire fleet of vehicles working and I worked very closely with these guys. This was a small group of people that were working on these vehicles every single day, with no break. At Abu Ghraib especially, there was always something coming in broken, had bullet holes or something that needed to be fixed."

After a few weeks of well-deserved family time and with reconstitution well underway, the focus was on the next deployment and for Walters and Edwards to go their separate ways. Walters recalled: "As the reconstitution was happening, I moved into a change of command, another LTC came in behind me and we swapped out. After that, we went back to the States, and I went to Squadron Command and was then deployed in August to Afghanistan."

Edwards added: "My next deployment was a little bit later. I stayed on in Germany after Bob changed command to help my executive officer replacement assimilate to the role. I stayed with him until the early

Major Edwards and wife Dana at the 165th Ball, Darmstadt, 2004, post Iraq (William Edwards' collection).

fall of 2004, then I went down to the U.S. Army Europe Command head-quarters and then went to Italy. The first job I was given was to organize, plan and execute the intelligence exercise for the Southern European Task Force mission readiness exercise, which was great, because I had just come out of theater with the 165th and then I was able to help train them from an intelligence perspective for their upcoming deployment in Afghanistan."

◆◆◆

As one of history's most vile institutions, Abu Ghraib was opened in the 1950s, operating in the capacity of a maximum-security facility and soon gained a reputation for regular executions and torture, amidst putrid living conditions for the inmates. In 2014, the Iraqi government closed down Abu Ghraib prison, ironically, citing 'Security concerns.' Major Edwards reflected on the closure: "Did it take that long? Seriously? That was way too long." Walters added: "That place should have closed down long before. A lot of the buildings that were there when we

LTC Walters and wife Nancy at a military ball, 2004, post Iraq (Robert Walters' collection).

arrived were in a state of complete disrepair. We had to build an infra-structure within the existing infrastructure and the only reason we did that is because we could not get permission to just level the place and move somewhere else.

"We should have never used Abu Ghraib in the first place. That's my opinion and that's what I told my boss back then. I said, 'We don't need this facility. This place is notorious from Saddam Hussein. Abu Ghraib has a very bad reputation, particularly amongst the Shias in Iraq, because of what Hussein allowed to happen there. By us coming in and using it, it associates us with him. We can't separate ourselves from Abu Ghraib and all the horror stories prior to that in the same spot. It gets smudged together and that's not a good thing for the U.S. Army.'

"Separating it in some place totally different made more sense. We could have taken everything that was there as far as the detainees and move it out in the middle of the desert some place and establish a detention facility, which is actually what we did at a later point and Bill ended up commanding it. Also, a different venue would have been more defendable because you weren't getting thirty rounds in ninety seconds on you because you could not return fire. In Abu Ghraib, we would get high explosive mortar fire and we could only shoot back illumination rounds, because it was located in a populated area and we didn't fire indiscriminately in populated areas. It made no sense for us to be there, but, for whatever reason, a decision was made at a higher echelon and we were not allowed to do that at the time. When it closed in 2014, I was happy and at no point should we ever go back in there and set up any operation as far as the U.S. Army goes."

For a number of reasons, many believed there was resentment from the Iraqis towards the U.S. after the initial invasion. Walters helped to clarify the opinion: "I did another year in Iraq as a brigade commander later on and after that, several special operations deployments. The Iraqis were resentful of us, and only in my opinion and experience, more so in the way we treated the Iraqi Army, because we dissolved it. I never got the impression they were mad at us because weapons of mass destruction were never found. In the Iraqi Army, the leaders were all Sunni, so when we first went in, the Shia were very happy because Saddam Hussein had oppressed the majority for his entire rule and so, the Shias were very supportive of us.

"What we did is, we didn't just leave after Saddam Hussein was cap-tured and I think the resentment is more from their perception that we were there to occupy them. When you go into a war environment like that, there's a lot of bullets flying and unfortunately, there are incidents of collateral damage where non-combatants are killed, not by design, but it happens in those highly kinetic infused environments that we found ourselves in. They resented us in our capacity as an occupying force.

"Some people were frustrated, that looting was taking place and we didn't do anything, but the reality is, we didn't have the authority to be Iraqi police officers. Those questions were posed and answered at the senior levels, but the bottom line remained, that was down to the Iraqis to control that."

Edwards added: "It was a lawless environment. There was no police and no structure. It was literally a free for all. Later on when I was back in Iraq from 2009–2011 timeframe, we were in the south of Iraq, but there wasn't that day to day contested environment you had in the Sunni triangle. Around the time of Abu Ghraib and shortly after, being an American soldier was far more challenging."

A true reflection of the popularity of any destination is reflected by the number of visitors it receives. While Camp Victory had the rich and the famous visiting on a regular basis, Abu Ghraib was far from a holiday destination and one which was served by many high-ranking officials. Walters explained: "On one of my last deployments, in Afghanistan around 2016–17, we did get some senior military and senior civilians. We had two Senators visit and other congressional leaders visit. But at Abu Ghraib, we didn't have any dignitaries come into the 165th tactical operations center.

"Abu Ghraib would not be considered a safe environment for a dignitary to visit, simply because of all the incoming fire. Where we were located, adjacent to Ramadi and Fallujah, was a hot spot in the area for Sunni radical extremist activity. During my other deployments, that was not always the case, for example, when I was in Bosnia in 1996 when the First Lady came over there. As you may remember, in the 2016 elections, she recalled when she was under fire when she landed at Tuzla Air Base. I was telling my wife Nancy at the time, 'That's totally inaccurate.' She said, 'What do you mean?' I replied, 'I was at the airport the day she arrived and there was no fire whatsoever. She got off the aircraft and was shaking hands with the party leadership that was there to meet her!'"

BusinessInsider.com wrote on June 23, 2016: "A false claim that

Hillary Clinton made while campaigning for president in 2008 is coming back to haunt her in the 2016 election cycle."

◆◆◆

Incredibly, after decades of service in the U.S. Army, including exposure to several combat deployments neither officer sustained any serious injuries. Edwards commented: "I was never wounded, thankfully. At Abu Ghraib especially, if you bear in mind the level of attack we were under, the majority of us were very lucky us to walk away with our lives. A lot of it also goes back to good discipline."

Walters added: "I agree with Bill regarding discipline. Overall, during my career, I was never shot or hurt from any form of incoming fire. The only time I came close was in 2008 when I was a brigade commander. I was up at the forward operating base at Camp Sykes, and was visiting the Rabia port of entry, which was an access point from Iraq to Syria, from Western Iraq. I had soldiers deployed throughout the Al Jazeera desert and would go up there and check on my guys. As we were departing the port of entry, we were ambushed. We were in a small convoy of three vehicles and I was in the lead vehicle, which was a large up-armored, mine-resistant ambush protected vehicle. So when the IED went off, it bounced me around the back of the vehicle a little bit, but didn't do more than rattle our cage thankfully.

"We received small arms fire right after the IED went off and even though our gunner was also rattled, he was still able to return fire with our 50 caliber machine gun. In fact, all three gunners from the vehicles turned and started shooting at where the small arms fire was coming from and the enemy dispersed rapidly. Other than that, I've had nothing that merited a combat injury."

Neither Edwards nor Walters embraced their fortunes lightly, nor did the United States Army. In 2005, alongside the 165th Battalion both men were awarded the Bronze Star for combat service, in recognition of their entire deployment in Iraq. In addition, they were also decorated with the Combat Action Badge, an award presented to soldiers who have been under direct or indirect fire by the enemy and have engaged in return fire. The latter award was given in recognition of the episode which took place in January 2004, where the battalion came under a barrage of nonstop rockets and mortars. Edwards recalled: "We were in Heidelberg for the ceremony. The general and all the senior officers all came in and participated. They pinned the badge on me and read the citation of what it was for. That's when Madeline first heard about Abu Ghraib from a more serious perspective. The full impact of what we'd been through in Abu Ghraib and the Sunni triangle really didn't hit me at the time. A few months after we left the whole Fallujah episode blew up and we were in full combat operations over there, which wasn't very far from Abu Ghraib. About four kilometers away."

Dana added. "After the ceremony, Madeline cried because she realized what danger Bill had been in and up until that point she had tried not to focus on it."

Post Abu Ghraib, Edwards dedicated a further fourteen years to the U.S. Army and Walters a further fifteen. The long list of awards they proudly had bestowed upon them, are now present on their Army jackets.

Through hard work and dedication, Edwards progressed to the rank of Colonel, effectively directing teams through a number of missions and projects. Undeterred by Abu Ghraib, he returned to Iraq in 2010 as battalion commander and chief operating officer, overseeing an operational environment that included two forward operating base commands 300km apart simultaneously, brigade combat team route clearance network defeat operations, key leader engagements with tribal and government leaders, diverse range of governance, economic development and security readiness programs. COL Edwards transferred the forward operating base at Camp Bucca to the Iraqi government, one of the first large base transfers, in December 2010 with the key responsibility and partnership with the Governor of Basra Province. This would begin the transition of authority that we would see in the end of 2011 as the U.S. ended major combat operations in the country.

In his final post, Edwards took on the role as Director of Intelligence for Theater of Special Operations Command North (TSOC) in Colorado Springs. During this tour he was charged with standing up a functional intelligence team and was an integral part of the United States Special Operations Command TSOC construct. In addition to a number of vital responsibilities in the role, he was the lead counter terrorism intelligence director for the area of responsibility designated through the combatant command.

Edwards recalled: "When Bob was the United States special operations command director of intelligence, I was a theater special operations command security officer, so we had the opportunity to work together again because we were in the same organization and both working intelligence. I was in a theater unit and Bob was the higher level up, but we were both intelligence officers at the same time."

Walters added: "Bill's boss was a Navy Seal who I served with and became good friends with.

"Then, down the line, when that commander was looking to hire an intelligence officer at the TSOC he reached out to me about Bill, because Bill was one of the candidates. The commander said, 'This guy doesn't have a lot of special operations experience.' I said, 'Don't worry about it. What you need is a superb intelligence officer and Bill Edwards is that guy. You hire him and you will not be sorry.' And he wasn't."

Edwards recalled: "There was no way I was going to get that job without that recommendation. The commander asked me to come up to Colorado and interview. I came up and went into his office and there was one chair sitting in front of this desk which was for me. I sat down and he brought in the entire leadership of the TSOC to stand behind me. The sergeant major, the chief of staff, all the colonels. They all start firing questions at me and I answered as best as I could. After they were done, the commander said to his team, 'You can all leave.' I got up and said, 'Sir. It was nice meeting you. Thanks for your time.' As I was walking out he said, 'Hey. Come here.' I walked back over to the desk and he handed me a coin and a flash for my beret and said, 'Welcome to the unit.'"

After thirty years' service in the U.S. Army, COL Edwards retired in January 2018. He now lends his immense skill base to those in need of protective design and security solutions. He is recognized as one of the world's premier experts in the field, consulting for some of the biggest and best known corporate entities, worldwide.

Following Abu Ghraib, Walters extended his promotional trail to the esteemed rank of Major General (MG). From 2004 through 2017, under the banners of Operation Iraqi Freedom and Operation Enduring Freedom, Walters spent a great deal of time immersed in Iraq and Afghanistan, supporting teams as part of an effort to counter insurgency and terrorism and help facilitate freedom to the residents of the respective countries.

After thirty-eight years and two months of service, on November 1, 2019, General Walters retired from the U.S. Army. His last post was as commanding general at the U.S. Army Intelligence Center of Excellence and Fort Huachuca, where he helped to provide executive leadership to an accredited academic institution that produced ten thousand graduates annually and operated with an annual operating budget in excess of $200 million.

Since retirement, Walters has become a highly qualified expert/senior mentor for the Army's mission command training program, training brigade, division and corps staffs on military decision-making processes and helping to prepare them for their pending deployments.

Edwards reflected on retirement: "At the time, I was what they call a 'Full Bird Colonel' and was working in a really great job at the TSOC. I had the lead for theater intelligence, but I was getting to the point where it was time to retire, time to transition. I tell people all the time, I didn't really retire, I just completed my military obligation. They tell you, 'You'll know when you're ready to retire and if you are there you need to go. By that stage, I was ready to retire. The funny part about retiring is when I finally let the unit know, the first thing that came out of their mouths was, 'Okay Bill. But don't cry at your ceremony!'"

"For me, the ceremony wasn't melancholy. I didn't write a speech, but in my head I'd been through a number of times what I was going to say. On the day, I wanted to talk about people that I knew and the ones that we'd lost. That was important to me. I

Major Edwards (Colonel by this point) shares a proud moment with daughter Elise, at his retirement ceremony (William Edwards' collection).

went back in time to when I was a cadet instructor and one of my cadets who became a Lieutenant eventually, but was tragically killed in Iraq. I also spoke about Specialist Karol, which at times became tough.

"Having Dana, Madeline and Elise there was great, because it was really a celebration of all of us. I wouldn't be a successful Army officer if I didn't have Dana by my side and doing everything an Army spouse does, in the senior officer ranks."

Dana added: "It was a great day, but for me, it was very surreal. Listening to Bill's speech, I couldn't believe this was the lifestyle we'd lived through as a family. I was actually quite relieved knowing that he was retiring."

Daughter Madeline recalled: "At that ceremony, there was a lot of detail about what he'd been through and that was very upsetting. My dad would tell us a lot of war stories, but they were always dark humor stories. We had an idea of what he was doing, but he'd always try and put a positive spin on it. Hearing him speak at his retirement was tough to listen at times, but I was very proud of him as a soldier and a father."

Sister Elise added: "I can't believe the things that he's seen, the horrors and everything he's been exposed to and how well he holds himself. I'm very proud of my dad. I have this person in my life who wants to protect people and has the best intentions behind it. I have always admired his motives of serving and I feel like the same kind of change is not possible in a typical civilian career. He's a natural protector and his heart is so good and I've got a lot of pride for everything he's done in the military. One time he told me that the moment I was born that he knew he would do anything for me. My dad always made me feel safe and loved. As a young woman now, I value his example of what a great man is."

Walters commented: "I didn't attend Bill's ceremony unfortunately. I'd just got back from Afghanistan and was the commanding general in Fort Huachuca."

Almost two years after Edwards retired, Walters recalled his departure from the U.S. Army: "My retirement was timed in conjunction with my change of command as the commanding general at the Intel Center and Fort Huachuca in Arizona. Bill was there and I really appreciated him making the trek to come down and participate. As I recall, we had a brief retirement ceremony under a gazebo and a Lieutenant General who was the presiding officer, said some nice words, gave me a medal, gave Nancy recognition and plaques from the Chief of Staff Army and that sort of thing. Then we walked over and conducted the change of command all at the same time. I didn't want to have something separate, because it required a lot of administration and organization.

"As for my remarks, there was a lot of effort put into the organization, so I thanked those folks. I thought when I was writing the speech, what do I want to say as I'm walking off the parade field with Nancy after thirty-eight years in the Army? Then I remembered this story about meeting an elderly lady at the airport in Washington, D.C., at Reagan International a few weeks earlier.

"I was sitting at the gate waiting on a flight, when this elderly lady sat next to me and struck up a conversation about her trip. During the course of our chat she asked, 'What do you do for a living?' and I replied, 'I'm a soldier.' She said, 'Really. What service?' and I said, 'The United States Army.' She said, 'How long have you been a soldier?' I replied, 'This summer will be thirty-eight years.' She thought for a moment and then asked, 'Are you going to make it a career?' I respectfully answered, 'Perhaps.' Then she said, 'What made you want to serve in the Army for so long?' I thought about it for a moment and responded by saying, 'It comes down to seven things. Loyalty, duty, respect, selfless service, honor, integrity and personal courage.' I explained to her, those are our Army Values that our soldiers believe in.

"When I think of loyalty, I think of a soldier, now a colonel, who deployed with me multiple times without complaint. Whenever I asked Matt to join the team, he dropped what he was doing and joined. Matt did not come alone, he brought his long time bride Kathy and their daughters. Kathy, an Army wife also demonstrated loyalty in that, during every deployment she was right by Nancy's side seeing to the needs of the families left behind and accompanying her to the hospitals when our wounded soldiers returned.

"When I think of duty, it is something we all do everyday, but some of us do it at a higher level. I am reminded of a young sergeant and the ambush in 2003 after infilling a long-range surveillance team. That soldier was awarded the Silver Star for valor and recognized by President Bush during a State of the Union address.

"When I think of respect, I think of my wife Nancy who goes out of her way to assist soldiers' families. Especially junior spouses. She frequently does it without identifying herself, but she does it to respect the sacrifice those young spouses are making being married to soldiers. To my high school sweetheart and wife, thank you Honey.

"When I think of selfless service, I think of a Senior Drill Sergeant who in 1987 was busy leading a company of advanced individual training troops here at Fort Huachuca but took the time to mentor a young lieutenant named Walters. He was in a position to drill troops and lead other drill instructors, but he took it upon himself to coach and train me. He retired as a command sergeant major.

"When I think of honor, I am reminded of a horrible night in August of 2011 when Extortion 1–7 was shot down in Afghanistan. Just three months prior, our unit was at an all-time high because we successfully executed Operation Neptune Spear and killed Osama bin Laden. Then, on the night of August 6, a Taliban fighter engaged one of our Chinook helicopters with a rocket propelled grenade and sent all thirty-eight SEALS, Afghan special operators and flight crew to a fiery death. Horrible. As we were preparing for the ramp ceremony to honor our dead, there was a tremendous push to conduct separate ramp ceremonies. One for the fallen U.S. service members and a separate one for the fallen Afghans; after all, it was an Afghan who shot down the helicopter. At the time, our commander patiently listened to the arguments, but decided, 'No. We will conduct one ceremony. We will honor all of those who fell that night, U.S. and Afghans alike.' And that is what we did. We honored them all.

"When I think of integrity, I am reminded of another former boss of mine who at the time was the commander of all forces in Afghanistan. He had been on a trip to Europe to speak at a conference when he and his team were delayed on their return to trip to Kabul. At a hotel, some of his staff were enjoying themselves in the hotel bar and made some disrespectful comments about the current administration within earshot of a *Rolling Stones* journalist. The commander was not present at the time of the incident. Later, when an article was published, the commander returned to Washington, D.C., reported to the president and took full responsibility for his staff's actions. He had the integrity to personally own it.

"Finally, when I think of personal courage I think of a young captain. One night, the captain was a pilot for the Night Stalkers of Task Force 160 and we were conducting a 'Command Underway' in the South China Sea. This is when a simulated terrorist element has taken control of a ship on the high seas and special operations forces are tasked to rescue the hostages. During that rescue mission, the helicopter assault force inserted the assaulters on the aft portion of the target vessel and upon the egress the flight lead suffered vertigo and the aircraft began to rapidly descend towards the ocean. Without hesitation, the captain took the controls, righted the aircraft and safely flew back to the float staging base, saving the aircraft and crew. The commanding general, in his report to the special operations commander stated, 'Sir, we had a successful training mission tonight without loss of life or equipment thanks to some courageous and extremely skillful flying despite the weather where the winds were strong, the seas were high, and the night was darker than my ex-wife's heart.'

"So, from sergeants and captains to colonels and all the way to generals who all personify Army values, that is why I have served so long. And at the end of the day, when I think of the words in Isaiah, 'Whom shall I send? And who will go for us?' And I said, 'Here I am, Send me!'"

Below is an excerpt of a letter daughter Martina wrote to her father for his retirement:

To say I am so proud of you is an understatement. I can't think of a more impactful phrase but please know I am grateful and honored to be your daughter. A daughter that is proud to be an Army brat who still uses phrases like 'You're a soup sandwich,' 'Roger,' 'Move with a purpose,' 'Adjust your shot group,' and probably most importantly gets goosebumps every time the national anthem is played or the Pledge of Allegiance is recited. I will always remember playing in the playground and stopping at dusk when the bugle sounded to lower the flag. Standing at attention with my fellow brats to show

LTC Walters (Major General by this point), walking off the field with wife, Nancy, after his retirement ceremony (Robert Walters' collection).

respect even if we couldn't see the flag. There remains a visceral reaction to others who don't show the same respect to our nation and a deep-seated desire to square them away on the matter. You have instilled a national pride in me but provided the opportunity to have a global awareness recognizing the world is a much smaller place than it can sometimes feel. Thank you for those experiences that included Scotch tasting in the glorious holy land of Scotland, those road trips with dryer vents duct taped to the A/C, visits to the mountains with roaring fires and most importantly slug days as a reminder to slow down every once in a while. Though there were tears each time the packers showed up, the Core 4 remained constant. I am thankful the Lord has allowed the Core 4 to be together as you hand off the baton and walk off that parade field with mom knowing you served well, you lead well and you loved your family well through it all.

Martina commented: "While 2003 was taxing, there were good times as well while dad was away. I have a picture in my hallway of the four of us from around 2012. We met at an Irish pub in Baltimore, because dad had to fly in for a meeting, my mom was in North Carolina at Fort Bragg where they were stationed, my sister was living in New York and I was in D.C. for work. We stayed for a few hours, had our Scotch and picked up right where we left off. I love that photo because we are laughing and it reminds me of our resiliency and ability to keep living our life the way we can, and coming together when we are able to."

Scotch in Baltimore for the Walters family, 2012. From left: Nancy, Daytona, Bob and Martina (Robert Walters' collection).

Team Walters still proudly "Embracing the Suck" in 2020. From left: Bob, Nancy, Daytona and Martina (Robert Walters' collection).

Daytona added: "Echoing Martina's comments—I wouldn't have traded how we were raised, where we were raised and with whom, for anything. Coming out of the events in 2003 made us much stronger."

Edwards concluded: "I was very fortunate to attend Bob's retirement and see a good friend finish a great career. There was about five hundred people in attendance, maybe more. It was an entire parade field. What was really touching was that when I told him I was coming down, he got me seated just next to the family section and we were all together, which was awesome. He gave those in the audience props along the way and mentioned me by name, talked about Abu Ghraib, the 165th and

Bill (left) and Bob reunited in Nov 2020— Bill just off his mountain bike enjoying retirement (William Edwards' collection).

mentioned about the 2003 ambush engagement. At this point, I'd been retired for a year and a half, my hair was long and I was wearing a suit. People looked around at me like, 'You were in that unit and went through all that in Abu Ghraib?' And I proudly thought to myself and nodded, 'Yeah. I was in that unit.'"

Index

Abdali 159
Afghanistan 20–22, 81–82, 92, 122, 166, 196–198, 200, 203, 205, 207
Alabama 6–7
Al-Asad 98
Al-Faw Palace 32–3
Al Jazeera desert 201
Al-Qaeda 19, 43, 128
Al Zarqawi 128
Amar 63, 65, 79, 87, 101, 103–104, 109–110, 137, 139
Amelia Island 6
Anbar 40, 110, 128, 152
Antwerp 195
Ash, Capt. Pete 4
Austin, Steve 124–125

Babenhausen 53
Babylon 73
Baghdad 13, 14, 28, 31–32, 39, 41, 43–44, 69, 72, 79, 95–96, 106–7, 112, 117, 124, 128, 136, 147, 155, 167, 189
Baghdad International Airport 31, 80, 117, 140, 148–149, 151
Balad 14, 20, 31, 33–34, 40, 44, 59, 66, 69–70, 72, 77–79, 81, 83, 87, 96–97, 100, 102–104, 106–112, 117, 121, 129, 134, 136, 145, 189
Basra Province 28, 202
Bedouin 35–36
Berlin 5
Berlin Frei University 5
Berlin Wall 5
Bin Laden, Osama 207
Blair, Tony (UK Prime minister) 29
Blue Cross Blue Shield 7
Bosnia 64, 107, 200
Bush, Pres. George W. 16, 21, 28–29, 206
BusinessInsider.com 200

California Lutheran University 3
Camp As Sayliyah 78
Camp Bondsteel 30
Camp Bucca 109, 160, 202
Camp Doha 20, 120, 159, 161, 164–165, 172
Camp Navistar 159–161
Camp Sykes 201
Camp Victory 32–33, 45, 124–125, 200
Camp Wolf 163–165, 175
Cena, John 124–125
Cheaha Mountain 7
Clinton, Hillary 201
Colombia 21
Combat Support Center Scania 142, 158–159
Combined Joint Task Force 7 45–46, 59, 74, 142, 167, 172

Darmstadt 22, 26, 55–57, 90–91, 97, 176–177, 190, 195
Daytona Erkan 22–27, 29, 49, 126–127, 177, 179, 181, 184, 210
Denmark 6
Dickens, Charles 189
Doha, Qatar 78
Dover, Delaware 99

E. Company, 51st Regiment 12
Edwards, Dana 5, 52–57, 85, 175–176, 182, 185, 190–192, 202, 205
Edwards, Elise 53, 56–57, 175, 180, 182, 184–186, 190, 192, 205
Edwards, Madeline 50, 53–57, 175, 180–186, 190, 192–193, 202, 205
800th Military Police Brigade 45, 48, 67, 167–168, 173
82nd Airborne Division 15 -17, Florida 6
Euphrates River 87, 120

Index

Fallujah 79–80, 128, 169, 200, 202
51st Infantry Regiment 12, 101
Firdos Square 136
1st Infantry Division 160
519th Military Intelligence Battalion 29, 46, 59, 168
Flentie, Mike (assistant operations officer) 9–11, 49, 68, 71, 81, 96, 117–121, 126, 130, 165
Fort Bragg 20, 29–30, 59, 69, 209
Fort Gordon 145
Fort Hood 21
Fort Huachuca 180, 203, 205, 207
Fort Leavenworth 7, 30, 190
Fort Riley 54
4th Infantry Division 136
Frankfurt 6, 31, 52, 176
Freedom's Sentinel 21

Geneva Convention 167
German American Tennis Club 5
Germany 7, 21–27, 29–32, 47, 49–50, 52–53, 55–58, 63, 68, 75, 89, 91–92, 94, 97–98, 120, 126, 134–137, 139–140, 145–148, 152, 161–162, 166, 173, 175–177, 182, 184, 190, 193, 195, 197
Green Zone 40–41, 43
Guantanamo Bay 48
Gulf of Mexico 6
Gulf War 20–21, 30

Heidelberg 32, 52, 55, 182, 201
Hussein, Qusay 39
Hussein, Saddam 10–11, 21, 28–29–30, 32, 39–40, 42, 60–61, 65, 104, 112, 128, 136–137, 156, 162, 167, 199

ISIS 21, 128

Jacksonville State University 6–7
Jordanian embassy 43

Kabul 207
Kansas 7–8, 26–27, 31
Karbala 128
Karkh 40
Karol, Specialist Spencer T. 97–101, 205
Korea 5, 21, 29, 109
Kosovo 30, 107, 176–177
Kurds 128
Kuwait 20, 29–30, 36, 69, 81, 95, 109, 119–120, 122, 134–135, 146, 152, 155, 158–163, 165–166, 172, 175, 177
Kuwaiti International Airport 164

Landstuhl 90, 92
Langen 30, 55–56, 176
Leavenworth High School 7
Lower Manhattan 19

MacDill Air Force Base 122
Main Supply Route, Tampa 33, 96, 148, 172
Malek, Martina 7–8, 22, 26, 29, 50–52, 179, 181, 193, 208–210
Maryland 181
MEDEVAC 14 -17, 86, 90, 96, 126, 139, 141, 144
Mosul 39, 107
Muhamed 63, 65, 79, 87, 101, 103–105, 110, 137, 139, 162

Najaf 35, 69, 128
Nasiriyah 158, 160
Naval Air Station, Miramar 5
New York Times 19, 48
The New Yorker 173
9/11 20–21, 91, 180–181; *see also* September 11
North Carolina 59

101st Airborne Division 40
160th Special Operations Aviation Regiment 129
165th Military Intelligence Battalion 2, 9, 12, 20, 29–31, 34, 40, 44–47, 52, 58, 62, 65–68, 70–71, 73, 75, 77, 80, 89, 102, 105, 111, 117, 124, 127, 129, 137, 144, 147, 152, 154, 166, 170–173, 175, 177, 195, 198, 200–201, 210
Objective Rams 35–36
Operation Desert Shield 20, 69, 95, 165, 179–180
Operation Desert Storm 5, 20, 55, 69, 95, 165, 179–180
Operation Enduring Freedom 203
Operation Inherent Resolve 21
Operation Iraqi Freedom 1 20–22, 29, 32, 50, 52–53, 55, 69, 179, 184, 187, 189–190, 193
Operation Neptune Spear 207
Operation Resolute Support 21

Pacific 5
Pennsylvania 19
Pentagon 19–20
Persian War 29
Peterson, Master Sergeant 7

Index

Port of Shuiaba 163, 166
PTSD 25 -26, 193

Qureishi, Capt. Romeo 32, 62–65, 71, 79, 83, 101–102, 104, 106–109, 112–113, 117, 122, 137, 142, 146–152, 158, 161–163, 165–166, 169

Rabia Port of Entry 201
Ramadi 41, 44, 79, 87, 112, 128, 200
Rasheed Hotel 43
Rhein-Main Airbase 31, 175–176
Ring of Cancer 159; *see also* Sunni Triangle

Saigon 5; *see also* Vietnam
Saudi Arabia 30, 69
September 11 19 *see also* 9/11
Shia 128, 199
60 Minutes 173
Socialist Worker Online 22
Soleimani, Qasem 149
The Sopranos 14, 111
Southern European Task Force mission 198
Spanish American War 5
Special Operational Joint Task Force 7 40
Sunni 128, 199–200
Sunni Triangle 79, 128, 159, 200, 202; *see also* Ring of Cancer
Syria 201

Taguba Report 167
Taliban 207
Tallil airbase 160
Task Force 160 207
Tawhid wal-Jihad 128
Theater of Special Operations Command North (TSOC) 202–203

3rd Armoured Cavalry Regiment (ACR) 40–42, 112
3rd Infantry Division 35–36
320th Battalion 60–61
Tigris river 87, 120
Tikrit 79, 107
Turkish embassy 43
Turner Barracks 5
Tuzla Air Base 200
203rd Military Intelligence Battalion 101, 152, 154
205th Military Intelligence Brigade 30, 32, 45–46, 59–60, 70, 73, 96–97, 142

Uday Hussein 39
Umm Qasr 109
U.S. Army Reserve Military Police Brigade 8
United States Marine Corps 7
University of Tennessee 20, 95

V Corps 21, 32, 70, 101
Vietnam 5; *see also* Saigon

Walter Reed National Military Medical Center 91–92
Walters, Nancy 7–8, 22, 24, 26, 29, 48, 50–52, 55, 90–93, 126–127, 136, 183–184, 188, 191, 205
Wansee Lake 5
Weisbaden 23
West Point 177
Williams, Maj. Mickie 32–33, 43–46, 59–60, 76, 173
World Trade Center 20
World War I 189
World War II 5, 109, 189
WWE 124

CPSIA information can be obtained
at www.ICGtesting.com
Printed in the USA
LVHW041539120122
708314LV00005B/189

9 781476 686738